D0440811

queer *by* choice

queer *by* choice

Lesbians, Gay Men, and the Politics of Identity

Vera Whisman

ROUTLEDGE
New York and London

Published in 1996 by

Routledge
29 West 35th Street
New York, NY 10001

Published in Great Britain in 1996 by

Routledge
11 New Fetter Lane
London EC4P 4EE

Printed in the United States of America
Design: Jack Donner

Library of Congress Cataloging-in-Publication Data

Whisman, Vera.
     Queer by choice : lesbians, gay men, and the politics of identity / by
Vera Whisman.
       p.   cm.
     Includes bibliographical references and index.
     ISBN 0–415–91014–5.   ISBN 0–415–91015–3 (pbk.)
     1. Gays—Identity. 2. Gays—United States. 3. Gays—United States—
Interviews. I. Title
HQ76.3.U5W5   1995
305.9'0664—dc20
                                            94–44781
                                               CIP

to J.B.

Contents

Acknowledgments

The production of this book, which began in 1987 as a doctoral dissertation, has benefitted from the assistance and input of many individuals. None of it would have been possible without the generosity of the people I interviewed; they told me their stories, answered my questions, and have shared their lives with me and, ultimately, with you, the reader of this book. I was supported over the months I spent interviewing them with a Dean's Dissertation Fellowship from the Graduate School of Arts and Sciences at New York University.

The various drafts that eventually became *Queer by Choice* were improved by the suggestions of many careful readers; while I am solely responsible for the final text, the best of the book comes with the significant help of others. Kathleen Gerson showed me how to do qualitative research, by teaching me how to listen to an individual during an interview, and to a tape afterwards. Along with the other members of my dissertation committee at New York University, David Greenberg and Edwin Schur, Professor Gerson encouraged, advised, and pushed me; all gave many hours of their time to close readings of my drafts. Michael Kimmel helped me make a dissertation into a book. Jo Dixon, Berenice Fisher, John Gagnon, Irwin Goffman, Arlene Stein, Carol Sternhell, and Shari Woodard all read my work and gave me advice that clarified my thinking. Jayne Fargnoli, my editor at Routledge, strengthened the book immeasurably, and was delightful to work with besides. Thanks are due to others at Routledge: Anne Sanow, Matthew DeBord, and Ron Caldwell saw the book through some difficult times. I am particularly indebted to the members of my writing group: Ellen Garvey, Jane Hulzka, Harriet Jackson, Ellie Kellman, and Nancy Robertson. Their rigorous readings improved every chapter, their encouragement got me through the process, and their friendship continues to bring me joy.

Martin Levine took me under his wing the day we met and never stopped nurturing me until the day he died. Marty was a mentor with a mission, a queen with a wicked sense of humor, and a courageous and generous human being. I miss him.

My family gave me their love and patience. To my parents, Lynn and Carley, and my siblings, Dona and Bob, I owe a lifetime of gratitude. And to my life partner Shari Woodard, I owe my every happiness.

Ithaca, New York 1995

one

Dear Abby, "The Gay Agenda," and the New York Times

In October of 1992, just in time for the referenda on Amendment 2 in Colorado and Measure 9 in Oregon,[1] a right-wing Christian organization called "The Report" released a twenty-minute video entitled "The Gay Agenda" (The Report 1993; orig. 1992). It is a slick and manipulative piece of anti-gay propaganda that may have been seen by a few hundred thousand people in showings on cable television and in church basements, Congress, and the Pentagon. Its distributors handed it out free by the dozens during the Oregon and Colorado campaigns, and its makers claim that 70,000 copies have been distributed.[2] The video's centerpiece is carefully selected footage from the New York and San Francisco gay pride parades showing precisely those spectacles most likely to shock a conservatively religious, nonurban audience: public partial nudity (with a particular emphasis on bare-breasted women), costumed portrayals of s/m scenes, drag queens (including San Francisco's Sisters of Perpetual Indulgence in their nuns' habits), and tender, affectionate, open-mouthed kisses between men.

"The Gay Agenda" is notorious for the claim its parade footage is employed to make: that the real agenda of the gay and lesbian movement is to force a perverse and public sexuality on U.S. society. But the video narrative also contends that homosexuals do not qualify for civil-rights protection because homosexuality is a choice. This second point is made in testimony from far-right ideologues acting as legal and medical experts, one of whom (Stanley

Monteith, M.D., author of a vicious treatise on AIDS) refers to young gay men as "boys being actively recruited out of our homes, out of our schools." Two men appear repeatedly who say they are ex-homosexuals,[3] and psychologist John Nicolosi, who has made a career of claiming to cure homosexuality, tells the audience that his work is central to the mission of the anti-gay backlash:

> The gay movement today is very much threatened by the kind of therapy that I do, because the therapy that I do can demonstrate that people can change. And it's essential to the gay movement that it convinces American society that homosexuality cannot change; that a person is born gay; there is nothing they can do about it but to accept it. So when you have individuals who can say, "I was once gay, but am no longer"—some of them move on to marriage, you know, and have a family—then that threatens the assumption of the gay movement. (The Report 1993)

Although most gay activists would doubt Nicolosi's claims of "success," and be offended by the very idea that homosexuality needs "curing," many would agree with his depiction of the public discourse about the legitimacy of homosexuality: In this view, the ability of lesbians, gay men, and bisexuals to win legal protection, cultural recognition and social acceptance rests on the claim that "homosexuality cannot change, that a person is born gay."[4]

When, in 1991, two researchers separately released preliminary findings suggesting that homosexuality may be biologically based,[5] they framed their claims in just such terms, utilizing Western culture's understanding of biological causation as the antithesis of individual intent. Medical psychiatrist Richard Pillard, coauthor of one of the studies, pronounced that "a genetic component in sexual orientation says, 'This is not a fault, and it's not your fault'" (Gelman, et al. 1992). Some gay activists hailed the promise of biological redemption; Randy Shilts concluded that proving homosexuality is innate "would reduce being gay to something like being left-handed, which is in fact all that it is" (Gelman, et al. 1992). Dean Hamer, whose 1993 research cautiously claimed to have located a genetic predisposition for male homosexuality, sees its political use as "challeng[ing] those who say it's a choice" (D'Adesky 1994: 108). And for their part, the Christian right has attempted to discredit such findings, lobbying to stop funding for Hamer's "gay gene" research (D'Adesky 1994), and providing followers with material designed to rebut his findings (e.g., LaBarbera 1993b). But is it so simple? Will the lesbian, gay, and bisexual movement prevail if we can demonstrate that homosexuality is innate? Will the far-right backlash succeed if they can prove that it's not?

We need to analyze these arguments in order to understand what interests are truly served by them. This is all the more important as the discourse becomes more and more widespread, as open debate about the legitimacy of homosexuality gradually replaces silence in the political culture of heterosexism:

> The closet no longer reigns in solitary splendor as *the* metaphor for the political situation of gay men, lesbians, and bisexuals. Its door now opens directly onto the *areopagus,* the forum, the senate hearing room, the court of law—onto scenes of rational debate, public deliberation, and collective decisionmaking conducted under the aegis of reasonable discourse. The muse of rhetoric, if not her sister logic, presides. (Halley 1993: 1727)

The growth of the lesbian and gay political movements has brought not only homosexuality, but also homophobia out of the closet, forcing the latter to speak for itself, no longer able to rely on the unspoken assumptions that a snicker or an innuendo could once invoke. The temptation, now that the monster has reared its head, is to counter its every blow with a defense, as did the group of young men who carried signs in the 1993 March on Washington that read: "GAY MYTH #4: WE WANT TO CONVERT YOUR CHILD" and "GAY MYTH #9: WE'RE NOT ENTITLED TO EQUAL RIGHTS."

But the discourse of homophobia is opportunistic and mutable; it can only be resisted, never entirely falsified (although so many of its individual claims, such as widespread child molestation by gay men, are quite obviously false) (Halperin 1994). Homophobic attitudes are "strategies for meeting psychological needs," and do not arise solely from simple misinformation (Herek 1984: 7). We need to understand homophobic discourse in terms of its rhetorical strategy, not solely in terms of its truth or falsehood.

In a non-heterosexist society, the question of whether homosexuality is a choice would command little attention. But here and now the question matters very much, and in most of the settings—legal, cultural, interpersonal—where the legitimacy of homosexuality is debated, the lines are clearly drawn: Those who would argue against homosexuality claim it is chosen, while those who would argue for it claim it is not. The claim of "no choice" is to a pro-gay stance as the claim of "choice" is to an anti-gay one: a foundational argument. Anti-gay rhetoric uses the term "sexual preference" to imply choice, while pro-gay rhetoric uses "sexual orientation" to deny it.[6] Legal cases with gay-rights implications have featured expert testimony that homosexuality is an immutable characteristic (Minkowitz 1993; Wolinsky and Sherrill 1993). On the other side, former Vice President Dan Quayle opines that "in most cases [homosexuality] certainly is a choice" (DeWitt 1992), and "Focus on the Family" (a far-right Christian group that campaigned for Colorado's Amendment 2) claims that gay men and lesbians constitute "a group that has no reason for calling itself a group, apart from their chosen behavior" (Rabey 1993: 41).

The *New York Times*/CBS opinion poll made it official, demonstrating a correlation between the belief that homosexuality is a choice and a range of homophobic opinions (see Table 1). The *Times* analysis equates correlation with causation, claiming that the data show that beliefs about whether or not homosexuality is chosen "*shape* attitudes on everything from homosexuals in the military to gay life in general"[7] (Schmalz 1993: A14; emphasis added). In fact the poll also uncovered large differences of opinion based on gender, age, education, region, and religion, but the *Times* article included findings only on the *effects* of beliefs about choice.

The *Times* analysis treats individual opinions about the cause of homosexualilty as relatively neutral beliefs that, once adopted, happen to have consequences for political attitudes. But individuals often select their beliefs to match their politics; one *already* states a political opinion by stating that homosexuality is or is not a choice. Such statements can function as metonyms, standing in for basic statements about whether homosexuality is a legitimate way of life. In the following excerpt from a "Dear Abby" column, it functions exactly that way; Ms. Van Buren responds to a letter that states "a person can be decent, respectable, and lovable, and still be gay," by verifying that homosexuality is not a choice. The response would be a *non sequitur*—the original letter says nothing about the source of homosexuality—except that "not a choice" stands in here for "legitimate."

Dear Abby:

I feel compelled to respond to a recent column in which Charles Piper chided you for encouraging a man to keep his brother's deathbed promise. The dying Ray had asked his brother to tell their grandparents that he was gay. Mr. Piper felt that the brother had no obligation to keep his promise.... Contrary to Mr. Piper, you did not blow it, Abby. In fact, you gave the brother excellent advice. You said, "At the end, Ray wanted his grandparents to know that a person can be decent, respectable and lovable, and still be gay." THAT is the central issue here....

Linda in Milwaukee

Dear Linda:

Thank you, friend. I needed that. There are still many people who do not know that being gay or straight is not a choice. If anyone doubts it, simply ask, "When did you choose to go one way or the other?" (Van Buren 1993: C2)

The formula ("not a choice" = "legitimate") is not the pop columnist's unique creation. It may well have been used by at least some of the respondents to the *New York Times*/CBS opinion poll who, because they regard themselves as non-homophobic, selected the responses they believed were non-homophobic.[8]

Table 1: How the Public Views Gay Issues

How the Public Views Gay Issues

Do you think being homosexual is something people choose to be, or do you think it is something they cannot change?

Choose to be gay 44%

Can't change 43%

Don't know 13%

Total adults		Those who say homosexuality ...	
		Is a choice	cannot be changed

JOBS AND RIGHTS

78%	Say homosexuals should have equal rights in terms of job opportunities	69%	90%
42	Say it is necessary to pass laws to make sure homosexuals have equal rights	30	58
11	Object to having an airline pilot who is homosexual	18	4
49	Object to having a doctor who is homosexual	64	34
55	Object to having a homosexual as a child's elementary school teacher	71	39

PERSONAL JUDGMENTS

46	Say homosexual relations between consenting adults should be legal	32	62
36	Say homosexuality should be considered an acceptable alternative life style	18	57
55	Say homosexual relations between adults are morally wrong	78	30
43	Favor permitting homosexuals to serve in the military	32	54
34	Would permit their child to play at the home of a friend who lives with a homosexual parent	21	50
36	Would permit their child to watch a prime-time television situation comedy with homosexual characters in it	27	46

FAMILIARITY

22	Have a close friend or family member who is gay or lesbian	16	29

Source: *New York Times*, March 5, 1993, p. A14.

Of course, choice/no choice is not the only dialectic plotted on the anti-gay/pro-gay axis. Certainly sick/healthy, immoral/ moral, unnatural/natural would also stand in for anti-gay/pro-gay. But unlike these examples, "chosen" is a value-neutral term on its own. It is not immediately apparent why stating homosexuality is a choice is necessarily stating that homosexuality is illegitimate, but that valuation is explicit in stating that it is sick, immoral, and the like. The way claims about choice play out in discourses about homosexuality is particularly important. A recently published gay-affirmative book of "Answers to 300 of the Most Frequently Asked Questions about Gays and Lesbians" bears the title, *Is It a Choice?* (Marcus 1993), suggesting that this is *the* most frequently asked question. And those young men at the March on Washington who carried myth-bearing placards reserved for "MYTH #1," *WE HAVE A CHOICE.*

Why not simply proclaim that we don't and be done with it? I hope *Queer By Choice* will provide a complex answer to that question, which for now can be summed up in two parts. First, predicating the legitimacy of homosexuality on its not being a choice is profoundly heterosexist. The very wording of the *New York Times*/CBS poll's independent variable question—which asked whether homosexuality is something people "choose to be" or something they "cannot change"—demonstrates that heterosexist bias, relying on precisely the same logic as "The Gay Agenda": If it is possible for a gay person to change to straight, *and assuming that such a person would make that change if she or he could,* by *not* undergoing whatever is necessary to make that change, that person is choosing to remain gay (even if she or he did not choose to become gay in the first place). It is that reasoning that makes of "choice" and "change" oppositional terms, in the *Times* poll and in the rhetoric of the far right. If we argue against only the "possible to change" assertion, we leave unchallenged the more insidious assumption that it is desirable or necessary to do so. And to the extent that homosexuality is acceptable only if it is not chosen it remains stigmatized, illegitimate, deviant. Added to that logical weakness is an emotional one; as D'Emilio (1992) asks, "Do we really expect to bid for real power from a position of 'I can't help it'?" (187).

Second, the claim that homosexuality is legitimate because it is not chosen is androcentric, treating a common male experience as generically human. Apparently the vast majority of gay men in the U.S. do understand their homosexuality as an orientation they did not choose or create (Bell and Weinberg 1978; Epstein 1987; Harry 1984; Hart 1985; Weinberg and Williams 1974). But lesbian identities span a continuum, from a model of lesbian identity as a conscious political choice to a determinist model like that of most gay men (Bell and Weinberg 1978; Burch 1993; Ettore 1980; Golden 1987; Ponse 1978; Reback 1986). The "born that way" stance not only "lets the other side set the terms of the debate" in heterosexist terms, but "reflects the universal male experience in this culture, not the complexities of the lesbian world" (Van Gelder 1991).

Choice in Lesbian and Gay Identities

These claims—that homosexuality is or is not chosen, is or is not innate—are important beyond their function as political rhetoric. Gay men and lesbians understand themselves and their personal histories in these terms, experience their sexual desires as beyond or within their own control. These personal accounts must be respected; neither liberation nor scholarship would be served by dismissing them at the very historical moment when gay and lesbian voices are speaking for themselves. But respect does not preclude analysis, beginning with the recognition that lesbians and gay men experience their sexualities in a heterosexist and homophobic context.[9] That context forces us to explain ourselves, for ours is not the unquestioned, the unmarked, the center. The very fact that lesbians and gay men usually do take a position on the etiology of our sexualities is a measure of our stigmatization.

Such personal statements, then, function as accounts, discursive devices that serve to neutralize stigma (Schur 1979), "employed whenever an action is subjected to valuative inquiry" (Scott and Lyman 1968). Accounts of identity, far from being mere descriptions of experience, are devices which individuals select and use because of what they can do for one in the negotiation of a hostile world. In the coming-out stories told by lesbians and gay men, such as those elicited by the interviews I conducted, these accounts weave into personal narratives, the telling of which constitutes one of the rituals of modern gay and lesbian life.

This book analyzes such identity accounts, as heard in individual interviews with a volunteer sample of 39 lesbians and 33 gay men. The interviews, comprising mostly open-ended questions, lasted between two and four hours. I conducted and taped all the interviews, most of which took place in New York City between October 1987 and March 1988.[10] I used several techniques to recruit respondents, including distributing flyers, placing advertisements in gay and lesbian publications, and "snowballing" (asking interview respondents to tell others about the study). In addition to general calls for lesbian and gay volunteers, I made some specific efforts to locate people—particularly men—whose homosexuality they identified as chosen. I make no claims that this sample is statistically representative of the U.S. gay and lesbian population at large.

In a sample as small as this, it is impossible to examine the effects of a range of demographic variables; on the other hand, the advantage of a small sample is the access it provides to respondents' own constructions of the origins and meaning of their sexual identities. So I present demographic information here solely to describe the sample and illustrate its diversity, not to suggest that I will distinguish the effects of all these variables. Of the 72 lesbians and gay men interviewed for this book, 15 are people of color. Of the 57 white respondents, 12 are Jewish. The sample is more educated than the population at large, as some studies (Elliot 1994) suggest that the lesbian and gay population itself may be. Over half of the respondents had completed a four-year college degree, and nearly a quarter of the total had some graduate education as well. Nonetheless, I was able to interview a total of 13 people who had completed either a GED, a high-school diploma, or less than two years of college. In spite of their relatively high levels of education, respondents were employed in occupations that varied widely in status and income;[11] of the 57 who were employed full-time, 28 worked in clerical, service, or manual occupations, and 29 in technical, managerial, and professional jobs (most of the latter were teachers and social workers). The sample is disproportionately youthful, with three-quarters of the respondents aged 35 or younger, and only four over age 50.

Although New York City is one of the epicenters of gay and lesbian community life in the United States, not everyone in the sample is a migrant to the gay mecca; half the lesbians and a third of the gay men grew up in the New York metropolitan area. And although a gay person—particularly a middle-class white gay man—can lead a very gay-centered life in New York, respondents varied widely in their level of community involvement and the extent to which they were out in their neighborhoods, workplaces, and families of origin.

I have used pseudonyms for all respondents, and disguised other recognizable features of their lives, following the usual procedures of sociological research to protect participants' anonymity. Not all respondents, however, wanted to remain anonymous *as* lesbians and gay men. (See Appendix for more on sample characteristics.) All quotations herein appear in respondents' own words, which have been edited to facilitate their translation from a spoken to a written format.

My analysis of respondents' identity accounts is both qualitative and comparative. Sometimes I treat data collected in the interviews in the straightforward manner that survey data are usually treated: as transparent reports of a reality beyond the interview (particularly, in this case, of the past). This treatment allows me to compare such data as respondents' reports of how long a romantic relationship lasted, or how many sexual partners they have had. Issues about what it can mean to say that anything "really happened," to suggest that there is one true version of an event which a respondent may or may not report, are set aside. I have treated such reports *as* accurate accounts of certain types of past experience as long as they are internally consistent.[12]

Yet I also analyze the accounts for their meaning, and here assumptions that they tell the truth are set aside, as we treat the narrative itself, rather than the reality it represents, as the unit of analysis. The need to move between these opposing approaches to respondents' accounts reflects the dual nature of personal narratives.

> A life story is not merely a collection of past memories, nor is it fiction; it occupies an intermediate epistemological space between history and literature since, like the former, it is essentially indebted to a past that "happened" and, like the latter, it is able to make use of rhetorical techniques (Corradi, 1991).

I sometimes pause at the level of the narrative itself, asking what respondents mean, and on what assumptions that meaning rests. There I utilize the language and techniques of discourse analysis. Valverde (1991) has argued that three of literary criticism's methodological innovations are usefully applied to the analysis of social discourse: deconstruction, through which "the potentially rigid dichotomies elaborated through fixed differences are undermined"(178); the older mode of literary analysis, which studies rhetorical use of language, useful since "discourse that aims at persuading an audience and generating social action is often structured not so much through formal logic but through tropes"; (179) and narratology, which draws attention "to the ways in which the most unliterary of individuals carefully organize the potentially infinite number of events making up one's 'life' into a coherent story resembling other stories"(181).

Chapter Outline

In Chapter Two, I examine the themes that came up as respondents talked about the idea of choice and relate these to the forms similar themes take in public discourse about homosexuality. Chapter Three looks more closely at individual respondents' accounts of the role of choice in their own sexualities. In Chapter Four, I compare groups of respondents who use similar accounts in an effort to understand why individuals tell the story they tell; I'm particularly interested in whether different stories reflect different experiences. Although I discuss gender differences throughout, those differences are the primary focus of Chapter Five, where I look specifically at how accounts of choice function differently for lesbians and gay men. In Chapter Six I return to some of the themes introduced in this chapter and the next one, and make some political and theoretical recommendations.

Notes

1. Both Oregon's Measure 9 and Colorado's Amendment 2 sought to prohibit any state locality from enacting or enforcing measures that would bar discrimination on the basis of sexual orientation. Measure 9, which failed by a margin of 56% to 44%, also sought to officially define homosexuality as "abnormal, wrong, unnatural, and perverse." Colorado's Amendment 2 passed by a margin of 53% to 47%, and was overturned a year later by the state district court. The U.S. Supreme Court has agreed to hear the appeal.

2. This claim comes from the operators of The Report's toll-free number, where over a dozen different books and videos can be ordered—all of them on the topics of homosexuality and AIDS, and bearing titles such as "Sexual Orientation or Sexual Deviation, You Decide."

3. The men claim to have been changed by an organization called "Love in Action." Both this name and the theme of "cure" appear intended to offset the video's

message of hate, and thus appeal to those viewers whose Christian values are gentler.

4.   "Born gay" is not precisely the logical opposite of "chose to be gay," for one could well argue that sexual orientation is not biologically determined, yet is determined by factors beyond the individual's control nonetheless. The psychological essentialism that was popular at mid-century, claiming that distant fathers and powerful mothers create homosexual sons, has stood up poorly to rigorous testing (Bell, Weinberg and Hammersmith 1981) and so has all but disappeared as the new biological essentialism has risen to take its place.

5.   Simon LeVay, a neuroanatomist, studied the hypothalami of 41 cadavers, and found that a portion of that brain center was twice as large in the heterosexual males as in the homosexual males or heterosexual females. Psychologist Michael Bailey and psychiatrist Richard Pillard studied twins and found that if one of a pair of identical male twins is gay, the other is three times more likely to also be gay than if the twins are fraternal. Results of the two studies were released in 1991.

6.   State legal codes seem to use the terms interchangeably. I use both, but do not take them as substitutes for one another, a position I explain in Chapter Three.

7.   The same correlation is demonstrated in an earlier study (Ernulf, Innala and Whitam 1989) where the researchers caution that the magnitude of the effect on attitudes toward homosexuality of beliefs about its cause is small.

8.   Zicklin (1992) makes the same point about the earlier research of Ernulf, et al. (1989), which reached conclusions similar to those of the Times/CBS poll but received much less public attention. Also, see Herek (1985) for a discussion of the evidence that individuals' opinions on homosexuality are shaped by their own political identities.

9.   By "homophobia," I refer to anti-gay bigotry, as practiced individually and socially by heterosexuals and homosexuals alike; by "heterosexism," I refer to "a diverse set of social practices ... in which the homo/hetero binary distinction is at work whereby heterosexuality is privileged" (Plummer 1992: 19), i.e., where heterosexuality is unmarked while homosexuality is stigmatized. The terms are parallel to, and related to each other in the same way as are the terms "misogyny" and "androcentrism."

10. Some of this moment in modern gay and lesbian history: The 1987 National March on Washington (in which organizers estimate 600,000 people participated) has just taken place. The AIDS epidemic is in its fifth year and the test for HIV antibodies is relatively new. ACTUP is less than a year old, and Queer Nation and an organized bisexuality movement have yet to make their appearance.

11. Badgett's (1994) exploratory research suggests that gay men earn lower incomes than heterosexual men in spite of their higher educational levels. The incomes of lesbians do not differ significantly from those of heterosexual women, whose incomes are already low compared to those of men.

12. I ultimately chose not to use two interviews which were highly internally inconsistent.

two

The Pleasures and
Dangers of Choice

One of my first interviews was with Al Davis, a 31-year-old[1] Jewish gay man who is articulate and politically active. When we were finished, he asked me to tell him more about my research.

> VW: It's fairly open-ended at this point.... I'm asking about choice, because it is something that women sometimes report—"This is something I've chosen"—and it's something men hardly ever say. So that's one of the differences I wanted to look at.
>
> AD: Politically, I think the mention of choice is very dangerous. And I don't like voices out there saying that we chose to be, because I don't think we chose to be. I think the political costs of our proclaiming we chose to be, as opposed to chose to do, are enormous. I think that's just what Jesse Helms wants.
>
> VW: Some people have told me that part of what they want to say is that that's a perfectly reasonable choice to make.
>
> AD: Politically, my instincts say, you don't win that way. Because they say it's reasonable, while others say it's not. I think I've become more convinced over the years, in talking to so many people, mostly men, about when they knew they were gay, and particularly with the research that's been done on estrogen receptors in gay men, makes me think that there's much that's biological.[2]

On the subway home from Al's Greenwich Village apartment, I wrote in my notes that I was "feeling a little shaken." Was I doing something dangerous—playing into the hands of Jesse Helms—by asking lesbians and gay men about choosing to be gay? I tried reminding myself that another part of "what Jesse Helms wants" (with all that stands for) is for gay men and lesbians to regulate themselves in anticipation of his response, to see with his eyes instead of our own. But I also knew that my book (if it were not ignored) could be misinterpreted. While I sat on the subway my mind raced with the imagined voices of conservative talk-show hosts gleefully telling their audiences some distorted version of something I had written. In reality this book is unlikely to attract the attention of the far right, whose tastes run more to the sensational. But I share my ruminations on Al's comment now to underline the point that at this historical moment saying that homosexuality is a choice—even sometimes, for some people—is dangerous.

Dangers of Choice

Although Al's statement was the most pointed, many respondents emphasized the risks associated with the claim that homosexuality can be chosen. Some seemed to see danger in the word itself.

> I would think really that people are innately bisexual, and—wait! That would mean you had a choice! (*Laughs.*) (Vickie Norvell)

> I guess when women get to the time where, they, they—I don't want to use the word "choice"! I don't know why it bothers me, you know. (Thomas Labadan)

Vickie and Thomas were in danger of violating a taboo when they found they were about to use the word choice. As though they were about to touch a forbidden object, they quickly backed off.

If Vickie and Thomas refused to touch the word, Justine DiAngelo held on to its rhetorical opposite, the claim that one is "born gay." She is a working-class Italian-American lesbian whose family subjected her to mental and physical abuse for being gay. Here she refers in understated terms to how hard her life has been, ending with a statement of defiance.

> Being butch and being out is not the most popular perspective for a gay woman in this society, a society that is homophobic, and it's geared to hate women. Especially women who love other women. And I don't care—you're born gay.

"I don't care—you're born gay." In that statement Justine reveals the armor that has protected her through the years: her sense that being gay is as much a part of her as the color of her eyes, and inappropriate as a basis for judging her. No matter what this society dishes out she asserts who she is and will not—cannot—be forced to change. For Justine, the ultimate deterministic claim—"you're born gay"—is a weapon in her personal battle for decent treatment and self-respect.

Sometimes the argument is not between an out gay person and her family and society, but between an individual's internalized conception of the "generalized other" and the self. But it's the same argument. Noel Steinberg is a 29-year-old photographer from an upper-middle-class Jewish family. When he first began to recognize his sexual feelings for men, he felt guilty and unhappy about them. Coming to believe that his homosexuality was not a choice became the keystone of his eventual self-acceptance.

> I started to realize I was gay in high school, but I kept denying it and saying, "No, I can't be like that; this is the most horrible thing." I was very frightened and scared by it. That I could be like this, that I'm no good, that I'm not a normal person. Basically, I think as I get older, I've been empowered by knowing that I am gay, and even sometimes a faggot. I'm empowered by it; I'm not frightened by it. Initially, I felt so bad, but then I said, "I just feel it's something innate. I don't think of it as a choice." I really don't.

Noel performed the emotional and cognitive work necessary to bring into alignment his understanding of homosexuality and his sense of himself as a good and normal person. He used his belief that his homosexuality was not chosen to stop questioning himself, but to start questioning homophobic and heterosexist standards.

> You know, being gay has opened up other areas which over the years have made me think about a lot of things. It's made me reevaluate certain basic issues like, "What is normal?" And you know, what is normal for one person isn't for another.

In his initial judgment that he was both "not normal" and "no good," Noel was combining the concept of sickness with the concept of sin, a common conflation in homophobic discourse. On the face of it, the claim that homosexuality is both a disease and a willfully chosen behavior is inconsistent. But the underlying stance that homosexual people are inferior *is* consistent: If homosexuality is a disease we are constitutionally inferior; if it is a willfully chosen behavior we are morally inferior.

Whether or not one may be blamed for an illness, one may certainly be blamed for a sin—one of the strongest linkages between the stigmatization of homosexuality and the notion that it is a choice. John Chambers, a 23-year-old white drama student from Ohio, is the only person I interviewed who is deeply troubled by his homosexuality. Many report that they once felt guilt or shame, but only John is still racked with them. He cannot integrate a positive regard for his homosexuality with his strong Roman Catholic religious beliefs.

> By the end of high school, I knew I was gay. I was thinking, "I haven't had sex with a man so I'm not gay. It may be a feeling. Most people have feelings, but I've never done it." Until you do it, you can't be guilty of being it. When I was nineteen I had my first experience. The next morning, I was like, "I'm going to hell." ... I don't like saying I'm gay because I really don't want to be gay. If I had a choice, I wish I was heterosexual. To me being gay is only a weak—it's not a weakness as much as it is something that is not accepted by society and it is not making my life any easier. It doesn't make me feel any better about myself.

John feels he is guilty because he has sinned, and he has sinned because he has chosen to do so.

> I guess I've chosen to be gay because I put myself in situations where I'll meet men and I'll have relationships with men. I set myself up for it.

John's sense that he had not sinned until he actually acted on his desires for men is consistent with Catholicism's institutional policy on homosexuality, according to which "homosexual inclination is not sinful but 'objectively disordered,' whereas homogenital actions are an 'intrinsic moral evil'" (Goss 1993: 13). The church's official position requires celibacy for homosexuals, and defines those who would defy that demand as willfully sinful (Goss 1993). So it is precisely where John feels he has exercised choice that he is most vulnerable to guilt and self-loathing.

The comments of Justine DiAngelo, Noel Steinberg, and many others like them are consistent with the essentialist approach to gay and lesbian identity, to be sure. But lesbians and gay men do not hold these opinions or make these evaluations simply because they are consistent with received thought. Few respondents stated or implied that the idea of chosen homosexuality was nonsensical, an evaluation that might mean that it is inconsistent with what is "known" about gay men and lesbians. Most respondents were more specific in their negative evaluations of the concept. They consider it a dangerous foray into territory controlled by homophobic discourse. When they repudiate choice, they are saying something positive about homosexuality.

Respondents related anecdotes that illustrate how the claim that homosexuality is a choice had been used directly against them. Jessica Padilla, a working-class Latina who lives with her mother in the Bronx, explains how her mother uses the claim of choice to avoid sympathizing with her daughter's oppression as a lesbian.

> Many times, when I was really upset because of my bad experiences with being a lesbian, I'd say, "Why? Why was I born like this?" And then, my mother debates this. She says "You were not born like this. This is what you chose. So hey, this is the consequences, you know. You could've been with a guy." And "blah, blah, blah," the whole bit.

With her comment, "blah, blah, blah, the whole bit," Jessica recognizes her mother's rhetoric as prepackaged, clichéd. Jessica is right; in this story her mother articulates a widely held but often unspoken belief about "fairness": Making a choice places on an individual all responsibility for "the consequences."[3] If Jessica chose to be a lesbian, the reasoning goes, then she has no right to complain about her bad experiences with it. Jessica's mother has put her finger on what the U.S. Supreme Court has called "the basic concept of our system that legal burdens should bear some relationship to individual responsibility" (from the 1973 plurality opinion in *Frontiero v. Richardson*; see Halley 1994).

In the context of this "basic concept," pro-gay essentialism is "an exoneration strategy, describing gay men and lesbians as incapable of resisting their sexual orientation and thus not 'responsible' for it" (Halley 1994: 518; see also Epstein 1988). That strategy has become the major approach to pro-gay litigation, as Halley points out in her critique of this "argument from immutability." The Supreme Court's ruling in *Bowers v. Hardwick*, that laws criminalizing same-sex sodomy were constitutional, made it necessary for "gay-rights advocates to convince courts that sodomy alone does not define the class of gay men, lesbians, and bisexuals" (511). What most advocates have elected to argue is that the class comprising gay men, lesbians, and bisexuals is defined biologically; in this context, the claim that homosexuality is sometimes chosen appears to undercut pro-gay advocacy.

Like pro-gay litigators, many respondents link their "not a choice" stance to a claim that homosexuality is innate. Thirty percent of the women I interviewed and sixty percent of the men believe homosexuality is innate, claiming as Dan Bartlett does:

> It's not a decision anybody makes; you're just born that way.

Partly, the appeal of such claims to individuals is the same as the appeal to legal advocates. It places homosexuality beyond the realm of culpability. But perhaps more importantly, it invokes science, the discourse with the strongest hold on legitimacy.

As Al Davis portrays it in the quotation that opens this chapter, biological science is the final arbiter of truth.

VW: Some people have told me that part of what they want to say is that [homosexuality is] a perfectly reasonable choice to make.

AD: Politically, my instincts say, you don't win that way. Because they say it's reasonable, while others say it's not. I think I've become more convinced over the years, in talking to so many people, mostly men, about when they knew they were gay, and particularly with the research that's been done on estrogen receptors in gay men, makes me think that there's much that's biological.

Al's strategy for winning is one that bypasses the public debate in which "they say it's reasonable, while others say it's not," by invoking science as a neutral authority that can be employed to mediate political disputes with empirical evidence. If it worked, such a strategy would transform a very material struggle of status politics into an abstract debate that the side with the most compelling facts would win.

That strategy is based on the naïve assumption that political argument is about truth. But as Nardi (1993: B7) points out, "There is no scientific evidence that genetic findings about homosexuality will cause people to change their minds and endorse equal rights for lesbian and gay people." And Halley's examination of the legal record shows that such findings have not been convincing judges; rejection of biological arguments has even accompanied rulings in favor of the pro-gay position (such as in *Evans v. Romer*, in which a Colorado district court handed down an injunction against Amendment 2). Widespread misunderstanding on this point notwithstanding, "the pro-gay argument from immutability, when advanced as a legal claim, is not the silver bullet its proponents think" (519).

More deeply, the strategy of relying on science accepts the ideology that scientific rationality provides a truly objective way of knowing that stands apart from—and above—the biased realm of politics. As decades of research in the sociology of knowledge have demonstrated, science does not escape the realm of power at all; it merely exercises power in a different form. Sociological critics of the assumptions and uses of biological research on the etiology of homosexuality—scientific critiques of the methods and findings of such research aside—warn against relying on scientific authority. They point out the very real possibility that "the attempt to eliminate homosexuality is one direction toward which seeking after and finding what is thought to be a biological cause might lead" (Zicklin 1992: 14). Geneticist Dean Hamer's recent proposition—that patenting his research might protect future misuse of it—recognizes the problem but is unlikely to solve it (D'Adesky 1994). As recent discussions about the genetic basis of phenomena from alcoholism to cancer demonstrate, "increasingly it is the conjecture that a particular trait is genetically or biologically based, *not* that it is 'only cultural,' that seems to trigger an oestrus of manipulative fantasy in the technological institutions of the culture" (Sedgwick 1992: 26).

That a characteristic is innate does not mean it cannot be altered or prevented if the will exists to do so, and in the control of that will it is not scientific research but political struggle that will protect gay men, lesbians, and bisexuals.

As Halley points out, that political struggle takes place simultaneously on many fronts, public and private. And for individual lesbians and gay men, the claim that homosexuality is determined by factors beyond one's control is "often the *only* effective resource available to gay men, lesbians, and bisexuals seeking to persuade their parents, coworkers, and neighbors that they can love someone of the same sex and remain fully human" (567). In the quotation that follows, Eric Lehman, a middle-class Jewish gay man, slides easily from the subject of innate homosexuality to his own understanding of prejudice and tolerance.

> I like to tell people that I was born this way. All I know is that I'm this way now. I know I've always felt this way as long as I've been able to feel things. It shouldn't matter, it really shouldn't, because I think the world would be a little easier place to live if people would get over their prejudices. "So you like men; that's fine." You're black, you're Jewish, you're this, you're that, whatever, it's the same thing. It's a sexual minority rather than an ethnic minority.

Eric invokes a model of "gay ethnicity" that has been successfully used to constitute lesbians and gay men as a political "interest group," and to define homophobia as a form of prejudice similar to racial bigotry, anti-semitism, or misogyny. In some localities legislation has officially designated gay-bashing a hate crime, and denial of housing, employment, or public accomodation forms of illegal discrimination, borrowing directly from previous efforts to protect the civil rights of racial and ethnic minorities. But for all its apparent utility, the gay-ethnicity model is not without its critics.

As Epstein (1987) notes, the gay liberation movement that formed immediately after Stonewall did not always portray gay men and lesbians as an essential, ethnic, group, as this quotation from an early gay manifesto demonstrates.

> The reason so few of us are bisexual is because society made such a big stink about homosexuality that we got forced into seeing ourselves as either straight or non-straight.... We'll be gay until everyone has forgotten it's an issue. Then we'll begin to be complete. (Wittman 1992, orig. 1970: 331)

Politically, many gay liberationists were as interested in freeing the homosexual in everyone as improving the lot of the gay and lesbian minority. But that earlier "universalizing" stance (to use Sedgwick's (1991) terms) soon gave way to the "minoritizing" approach of the gay ethnicity model, seemingly hoist by its own petard: "Simply by advancing the cause of gay liberation, the liberationists helped to further the notion, among both gays and straights, that gays constitute a distinct social group with their own political and social interests" (Epstein 1987: 19). The movement that survived to form nationwide organizations prepared to do battle in the political mainstream, found the minoritizing approach provided for "appeals to the professed beliefs of the dominant culture, emphasizing traditional American values such as equality, fairness, and freedom from persecution" (38). In contrast, traditional American values provide no obvious hook on which to hang the claim that, as I put it to Al Davis, homosexuality is a perfectly reasonable choice to make.

Precisely because it fits so neatly into a political culture of liberal pluralism, the gay ethnicity model is limited. The ways in which homosexuality could be a force for substantial and radical social change are undercut by a formulation that does not truly criticize the dominance of heterosexuality. In the practice of such minority politics, "the work of challenging the hegemonic definitions of sexual normality is abandoned."

> [S]exual minorities by definition can never become majorities. The
> acceptance of homosexuality as a minority experience deliberately
> emphasizes the ghettoization of homosexual experience and by
> implication fails to interrogate the inevitability of heterosexuality.
> (Weeks 1985: 199)

The gay-ethnicity model's failure "to interrogate the inevitability of heterosexuality" distinguishes it from the lesbian-feminist model, which begins with that interrogation. According to lesbian-feminism, lesbians are primarily women who resist compulsory heterosexuality. "What is a lesbian?" asks "The Woman-Identified Woman," the original lesbian-feminist manifesto, "A lesbian is the rage of all women condensed to the point of explosion" (Radicalesbians 1992, orig. 1972: 172). By questioning the normality of heterosexuality, and valorizing lesbianism as "the primacy of women relating to women. . .which is at the heart of women's liberation," lesbian-feminists made of lesbianism no "mere sexual preference."

> If we think of heterosexuality as the "natural" emotional and sensual
> inclination for women, [lesbians' lives] are seen as deviant, as patho-
> logical, or as emotionally and sensually deprived. Or, in the more
> recent and permissive jargon, they are banalized as "life-styles." (Rich
> 1980: 652)

By positing a "lesbian continuum," "a range . . . of woman-identified experience," Rich emphasizes the universalizing tendencies of lesbian-feminism. Although she portrays gender in strictly dichotomous terms, she pictures the boundary between heterosexuality and lesbianism as one that can be easily crossed. By understanding sexual preference as potentially a choice, and the lesbian as Everywoman, lesbian-feminism rejects an ethnicity model of lesbian politics.

The gay-ethnicity model stands counter to lesbian-feminist ideas, and also actually portrays them as homophobic. Kitzinger (1987) finds that researchers situated in such a liberal gay-affirmative position have defined homophobia so that it is indicated by disagreement with statements such as the following:

- The basic difference between homosexuals and other people is only in their sexual behavior.
- Homosexuality is just as natural as heterosexuality.
- If laws against homosexuality were eliminated, the proportion of homosexuals in the population would probably remain the same.

In contrast, the lesbian-feminists Kitzinger surveyed tended to agree with statements such as the following:

- Being a lesbian is much more than having sex with women.
- Lesbianism is a blow against the patriarchy.

And they disagreed with the statements below:

- You cannot choose to be a lesbian; if you are, you are.
- Most women are, by nature, heterosexual.

She concludes that as long as the gay and lesbian movement understands its purpose as advocating the acceptance of a sexual minority it will avoid its more radical potential for broadening sexual and familial relationships beyond the nuclear family, a potential in which lesbians, and women in general, have the greatest stake.

Lesbians and gay men of color also lose out in the gay-ethnicity model. Some of the African-American respondents I interviewed pointed out ways in which the ethnicity/sexuality analogy breaks down.

I feel more oppressed as a black person. Because of the fact that I'm black, people will tune in to that sooner than they will my lesbianism. If you are a white gay person, you have the option of being out or not. But as a black woman, I don't have that option. I can't pass. (Claire Williams)

> Being gay is something you can hide, where you can't hide being black, so it's complicated. But being openly anti-gay is more popular than being openly racist. There are things people won't say about black people that they will say about gay people, and they'll say them more often because they don't know gay people are in the room. But because race and class are still bound up, the actual structures of oppression of black people tend to be more vicious in certain ways than the oppression of gay people. (Maurice Raymond)

Fernandez (1991) points out that the gay-ethnicity model is not only based on inaccurate analogies; it is at least implicitly racist. Noting the "irony of a white-led movement with limited racial consciousness turning around and appropriating ethnicity and the stigma of race as legitimating tools," (23) he explains that the movement's self-image as a quasi-ethnic minority is part of the process that puts gay men and lesbians of color in secondary, marginal positions in it.

> A gay person defines herself or himself exclusively in opposition to the category of heterosexual.... The struggle against homophobia and heterosexism becomes, then, the primary agenda for a movement toward liberation. It is a movement that cannot afford to waste energy fighting against other oppressions.... These views effectively shut out those among us whose personal and political ideologies are defined by more than simple opposition to heterosexuality.... [T]he lesbian and gay movement has narrowly defined its primary subject. (21–22)

Taken to its minoritizing extreme, the ethnicity model reduces potentially liberating movements to "fractious disenfranchised groups competing in the marketplace of rights, representation, and privileges," and posing "no great danger to the political and social system that oppresses us all" (23).

The minoritizing approach rests upon an essential difference between heterosexuals and homosexuals, and provides a reason for maintaining a clear boundary between the two. That may be one reason that some gay men and lesbians hold to very negative opinions of bisexuals and bisexuality. Although I did not solicit them, some respondents shared such opinions during our interviews. Two men suggest that bisexuality simply does not really exist.

> I know one person who is proudly bi, but I've never seen any evidence of that. He's sort of a joke in our group. He marches in the Gay Pride Parade with a t-shirt on that proclaims that he is bisexual and proud of it, but nobody has ever seen him with a woman. (*Laughs.*) (Walt Richardson)

A few more—men and women—share a belief that bisexuality is morally or psychologically suspect.

> I think calling yourself bisexual is the purest form of narcissism. It's like, "If it has an orifice, I'm gonna use it." (Sam Broome)

> I don't know that many people who claim they are bisexual, but to me it seems like you're not committing yourself. You know, like it's just sort of sitting on the fence. And I don't believe in that. (Alice Morgan)

Among politically active lesbians and gay men, particularly on college campuses, such opinions are now recognized as "biphobic," and have certainly declined in the relatively short time since these interviews.

Bisexuality threatens the sanctity of the hetero/homosexual divide, and undercuts the ethnicity model (Rust 1991; Udis-Kessler 1991). It is also strongly associated with choice; as Vickie Norvell, a white 28-year-old graduate student in history reminds herself.

> I would think really that people are innately bisexual, and—wait! That would mean you had a choice! (*Laughs*.)

But it is possible to recognize the political limitations of the gay ethnicity model—particularly the way it privileges white gay men over others in the lesbian, gay, and bisexual movement—and continue to recognize its relative effectiveness in the battle against homophobia and heterosexism. Essentialism does not permit gay and lesbian activists to frame the discussion of homosexuality in critical terms, but it does give them a way to participate as advocates.

> Our culture still sees to its being dangerous enough that women and men who find or fear they are homosexual, or are perceived by others to be so, are physically and mentally terrorized through the institutions of law, religion, psychotherapy, mass culture, medicine, the military, commerce and bureaucracy, and brute violence. Political progress on these and similar life-and-death issues has depended precisely on the strength of a minority-model gay activism. (Sedgwick 1991: 58)

When it works, ethnicity/minority-model politics can legally prohibit the majority from acting on its bigotries, which are ever in evidence. Thus Sedgwick suggests that we need to "underwrite continuously the legitimacy of both" minoritizing and universalizing approaches. It is to that end, and not to its obliteration, that the useful critique of the gay-ethnicity model proceeds.

While a claim that homosexuality cannot be chosen appeals to concepts of liberal politics, it also draws on historically specific understandings of sexuality and "human nature." These assumptions appear in respondents' discussions of choice as trivializing:

> I feel it's an innate thing; I don't feel this was a conscious decision. You know, all of a sudden I'm going to get up and you know, "I'm not going to eat this for breakfast any more; I'm going to have that." I think it went beyond that. Quite a bit beyond that. (Noel Steinberg)

> It's not just, "Oh, now I'm gonna have sex with Sally." I know people who've decided they're not gay anymore. I don't think you just decide to be gay, and I don't think you just decide not to be gay. (Ralph Myers)

> You know, when people talk about it being a choice, I really don't agree. I certainly don't feel like I sat and thought, "Well, I'd rather be a lesbian than a heterosexual." (Sharon Halpern)

> I know that making that kind of decision [to be a lesbian] without feeling that it was really tied in, in some more profound way, wouldn't work. (Karen McNally)

These statements differ from some of the previous quotations in that they do not directly answer a prominent claim of homophobic discourse: opponents of lesbians and gay men do not generally claim that we choose our sexual preference the way one chooses a breakfast cereal. So rather than respond to a homophobic claim, these statements undercut the entire homophobic rhetoric of choice. They draw on notions of choice as entirely inappropriate to matters of desire and emotion, which are matters of passion, not deliberation. They talk about a generalized sexual preference the way people talk about love for a particular person: We don't choose to love someone; we "fall" in love. These quotations—most of which use sarcasm—charge those who would claim that homosexuality is a choice with sheer stupidity, with a failure to understand what processes of the human psyche are and are not amenable to choice.

In making that distinction, these respondents follow a well-worn path in Western thought that describes human nature as essentially dual: on the one hand animalistic, savage, pleasure-driven; on the other civilized, moral, law-abiding. As Starbuck (1981) points out, both repressive and expressive theories locate sexuality in the first realm, subject to the inhibiting forces of society, located in the second: Mr. Hyde restrained by Dr. Jekyll. Repressive models from Christian morality to Freudian hydraulics accept the necessity of that restraint; expressive critiques mourn it while accepting the premise of duality.

Neither of these models would value a chosen homosexuality. Expressionists would hear a tale of natural desires willfully constrained; repressionists would hear that one has failed to do just that, that one has exercised the will to not regulate. But sometimes those who avow a chosen homosexuality are attempting to say something that neither of these approaches can hear, something that implicitly recognizes that those two aspects of human nature are ideas, not really separate, bounded regions (indeed, even their locations, the body and the mind, are not separable). Then, one can choose to be gay through a process that cannot be described as either repressive or expressive—a process that utilizes the continuity between mind and body, society and sex, rather than one that involves the victory of one over the other.

But in the quotations above, duality is alive and well; the speakers use it to marshall the forces of expression over those of repression. As they delineate it, deliberation and choice are for consumer products, for fads, for an overly rational approach to planning one's life. Love, sex, and desire "go quite a bit beyond" these mundane choices and, compared to these passions, the idea of choice itself appears to be dry, sterile, mechanical. That image of choice is the legacy of consumer capitalism, implicitly invoked in the statements above. When respondents reserve some part of their lives that is beyond the reaches of choice, they reserve a "haven in a heartless world," and seek to protect some part of themselves from bureaucratic instrumentality. In this effort, gay men and lesbians join a common effort to save such aspects of experience as love, sex, and family from capitalist social relations (Ehrenreich 1979, Ginsberg 1984).

In an advanced consumer capitalist economy, the concept of individual choice tends to depoliticize whatever it touches. For example, poverty is simply the outcome of freely but poorly made choices, and the key to understanding domestic violence is knowing why a battered spouse doesn't just choose to leave. Choice is the rhetorical vehicle by which public issues are transformed into private troubles, as C. Wright Mills (1959) put it, and radical social critics are rightly suspicious of it. Although she applauds the way the assertion of chosen lesbianism corrodes the boundary between lesbianism and female heterosexuality, Kitzinger (1993) balks at its use to ignore the ways that "heterosexuality and lesbianism are *not* equivalent options" (51). Mary Behnke's hesitance to use the term comes out of that awareness:

> Being heterosexual is not a choice. So if you can't freely choose that option to be heterosexual, how can you freely choose to be a lesbian? I guess that's my problem with "Is it a choice?"

Gendered Dangers

The claim of chosen homosexuality endangers men and women differently, since the manifestation of compulsory heterosexuality is gendered. Many of the gay men I interviewed responded to my questions about whether homosexuality can be chosen only in terms of choosing to become heterosexual. (None of the lesbians answered this way, a point to which we will return below.) Unfamiliar with the notion that anyone might choose to be gay, these men reinterpreted the questions in order to turn to the belief that gay people can choose to be straight, the only connection between choice and sexual preference with which they were familiar. Although these respondents do not mention anti-gay discourse directly, they share with the respondents quoted above an emphasis on the dangers associated with the idea of choice, by pointing out the strength of the assumption that the only choice a person would make is to be straight. They do not question that assumption; rather, they take the opposite side in an argument framed by it.

> VW: Do you know anybody who claims that they chose to be gay?
> SB: No. I know people who at times express a wish to not be, to choose not to be gay. But never to choose their [homosexuality]. I never heard of that. (Sam Broome)
>
> VW: Have you ever heard of the notion that gay identities are chosen, that people choose to be gay?
> TM: Not specifically, but I think that's what some religious fanatics think, that they could push a button and they'd be changed back to the correct way. (Terence Metcalf)

Malcolm Wilson, quoted below, reports that although it is difficult to accept the idea that being gay might be a choice, his ideas about choice have changed. Before the change his opinions might have looked much like those quoted above, and he still shifts immediately from the topic of choosing to be gay to the issue of choosing to be straight.

> I know that people do [choose to be gay]. I have friends who have. I didn't used to before, but now I sort of feel I can accept the idea that one could turn gay. Which I guess means that one could turn heterosexual, I suppose. I mean, on some of these talk shows you always see at least one person who will say, "I used to be gay and now I saw the light." What is going on? You start to think, well, is it really possible for the person to have *turned* heterosexual?

Malcolm articulates it most clearly, but Sam and Terence voice the same concern: If it is possible for even some people to choose to be gay, it must be possible for some to choose not to be. And that logical symmetry contrasts sharply the very real social asymmetry of the heterosexuality/homosexuality binary. The discourse on sexual preference is so thoroughly shaped by heterosexism that often the only use for the concept of choice is in the assumption that if individuals can choose their sexual preference they will choose heterosexuality. The association of "choice" with "change" (as in the wording of the *New York Times/ CBS* opinion poll—"Do you think being homosexual is something people choose to be, or do you think it's something they can change?") always posits a change from homosexuality to heterosexuality. For many years, homosexual men in particular were subjected to tortuous cures, often against their will. The American Psychiatric Association's 1973 deletion of homosexuality as a pathological diagnosis from its Diagnostic and Statistical Manual pushed such treatments to the psychiatric fringe, where today counseling organizations that seek to make gay people straight are often supported by Christian churches (Green 1993; LaBarbera 1993a). For children, however, such cures are situated in the medical mainstream. The treatment, nearly exclusively in boys, of "Gender Identity Disorder of Childhood" is a psychiatric effort to prevent homosexuality (Sedgwick 1992).

The coercion in this situation is so intense that it robs the term choice of its meaning. That is one reason respondents back away from the word: We do not make choices in a setting of "spacious emotional or analytic impartiality," but in a setting that features "urgent homophobic pressure to devalue one of the two nominally symmetrical forms of choice" (Sedgwick 1990: 9). And as such interventions were and are more commonly aimed at gay men than at lesbians, it is not surprising that for many gay male respondents the only connection between sexual preference and choice is the one that reflects "a culture's desire that gay people *not be*" (Sedgwick 1992: 26).

That culture's desire is most strongly that gay *men* not be, for it is gay men who are most often the targets of anti-gay violence, whether on the street or in the clinic. Paradoxically, the more direct targeting of gay men, compared to lesbians, is an outcome of male dominance. The stigmatization of male homosexuality provides a lever for keeping all men, whatever their sexual desires, behaving as dominants (see Blumenfeld 1992; Carrigan, Connell, and Lee 1985; Connell 1987; Herek 1987; Kinsman 1992). To call a man, especially a young one, "faggot" is to mark his masculinity as spoiled. Nonetheless, in a male-dominated society such as this, men have considerably more leeway in their behavior than women. They may even have sex with men under certain circumstances, most notably where they take only the dominant sexual position and do not become emotionally involved (see Blumstein and Schwartz 1976a, 1976b, 1977; DeMonteflores and Schultz 1978; Gagnon and Simon 1973; Humphreys 1970; Reiss 1961; Sagarin 1976). There is a great deal men may *do*, but they must not *be* gay. Heterosexuality requires of women nearly the opposite: They must be heterosexually available, but beyond that women's sexual *being* is of little import.

The gendered construction of compulsory heterosexuality creates differences in the ways lesbians and gay men think about choice. None of the lesbians I interviewed associated it only with the pressure to change and become heterosexual. Instead, most indicated that women who choose to be gay aren't real lesbians. Very few gay male respondents said anything about men who are gay by choice being unreal; a few of them did make such statements about women, as

Thomas does below. The "real" v. "false" issue is specifically lesbian, and is associated with a number of concerns. Some of the respondents suggested that a chosen sexual preference, as opposed to a determined one, could be temporary; their stories advise the listener not to trust a chosen lesbian to "keep going," as Cindy puts it, when her gay life gets tough.

> VW: Have you ever heard anybody say they chose to be gay or lesbian?
>
> TL: Oh, yeah. When I was in college, we did a panel. And there was one lesbian, and she said that [she had chosen to be a lesbian]. One student asked her, "Well, in your later life, would you want to have your own children, a family and all that?" "Oh, yes!" She stood there and said, "Oh, yes, I want to have my own kids, and probably have a husband." And "What?! …What is she talking about?!" (Thomas Labadan)

> There have been an occasional few, maybe like younger people, that I think have chosen to live like a lesbian, live as lesbians, but I don't think they're really lesbians, and I think that eventually they'll become heterosexual. Because I don't think they have the stamina to keep going. (Cindy Schwartz)

Some suggested that lesbians by choice were just heterosexual women who were pretending to be lesbians in order to be hip, "groovy."

> VW: Have you ever heard of the notion that lesbian and gay identities are chosen?
>
> AM: Well, yeah. But I kind of think that's a heterosexual construct, know what I mean? Like that makes them groovy or that makes them different, or that expresses their anger toward the opposite sex. (Alice Morgan)

For Alice, "false" lesbians are "really" heterosexual women. Others suggested that women who choose to be gay are not real lesbians because their true sexual orientation is bisexual. Neither Suzie nor Joy is "ready to accept" as lesbians women "who could go either way."

> My thought is there's some women who have chosen to be lesbians, who could go either way, really, and probably more so back in the seventies, really chose to be lesbians, and then there are other women who don't choose it, who *are* lesbians. And I think the ones who choose it are probably more so the ones who are now choosing to be with men. They're really, they're kind of bisexual. (Suzie Gluck)

I was amazed at how many young women—I don't think they're really homosexual—have chosen to be gay for some reason. I cannot figure it out and I am not ready to accept. I don't know why. I know there's a very very large bunch of people, a great number who are functioning bisexuals. That may be part of it. (Joy Levine)

For the respondents quoted above, lesbians by choice are not real because they have the wrong underlying sexual orientation, whether heterosexual or bisexual. For Vivienne, quoted below, it's the chosen lesbian's motivation—hatred of men—that is wrong. (Alice also mentions "anger toward the opposite sex" above.)

I know a couple who say it was because of this or that horrible experience with men, which I tend to not trust that much. Because if that's really the case, it's the wrong reason. You're a lesbian because you like women, not because you hate men. (Vivienne Medina)

To others, the concept of chosen homosexuality was nearly incomprehensible, because for real lesbians and gay men, "it's just there," "deep inside."

I don't see how a person can pick and choose. I mean, it's like a person likes spinach or doesn't like it. I don't think a person chooses not to like it. It's just there. You just eat it or not eat it. (Paula Weiss)

I really can't believe wholly that they could just turn off and switch. You know, that had to be in them somewhere, deep inside. (Jack Miklowicz)

VW: Do you know anybody who feels they made a conscious choice to be gay?
RB: Well, I know a lot of confused people—a few confused people. (Rhonda Barker)

These responses are deeply essentialist, and demonstrate a folk epistemology in which the truth will out: A false lesbian will eventually revert to her true heterosexuality, and a person who eventually becomes gay must have always been so inside. The knowledge in use here is positivist, portraying reality as "out there"—or, in this case, "in there." But there is more than essentialism behind the lesbian concern with realness. It's a concern that arises from the particular reality of lesbian life in this society, with pressures that have as much to do with sexism as with heterosexism.

The distinction between real and unreal lesbians takes its import from the androcentric construction of heterosexuality: The institution of heterosexuality is not constructed around female desire, so it doesn't depend on whether a woman would rather be with a man than with a woman. Indeed, the prevalence of rape and other forms of sexual coercion demonstrates that it does not always matter that a woman may not want to have sex with a particular man at a particular moment. As such, heterosexist pressure on lesbians is related to the treatment of all women as male sexual property, and is different from the heterosexist pressure on gay men. Add to this the economic coercion whereby marriage is often the alternative to poverty, and it is clear that even though verbal and violent harassment are aimed more at gay men than lesbians the coercion to behave heterosexually is intense for women. As such any woman who can—who is not simply unable to—relate sexually to men might succumb to the considerable coercion to do so. Therefore, she can't be trusted by women whose lesbianism is unchosen, unchanging, "real."

The distinction between real and unreal lesbians has been a feature of lesbian culture since at least the early twentieth century, when sexologists distinguished the "true invert" from her partner (Reback 1986). Havelock Ellis, for example, distinguished the "actively inverted woman," whose "essential character" is marked by "a more or less distinct trace of masculinity," from "the women to whom the actively inverted woman is most attracted," who differed from "normal" women in that they were "not repelled or disgusted by the lover-like advances from persons of their own sex" (1928: 222; see also Chauncey 1982–83).

Radclyffe Hall's 1928 novel, *The Well of Loneliness*, is the classic portrayal of the invert and her lover: The protagonist is a masculine woman whose lover is conventionally feminine, and heterosexual before and after their relationship. The distinction captures several dimensions: masculine *v.* feminine, determined *v.* elective, real *v.* false. Students of lesbian identity have emphasized these differently, characterizing the pairings as primary and elective lesbians (Ponse 1978), born and chosen lesbians (Ettore 1980), and exclusive and bisexual lesbians (Burch, 1993). These distinctions overlap but do not eclipse the distinctions between butch and femme. In the butch/femme lesbian communities of the mid-twentieth century, femmes were sometimes characterized as women who could—and so therefore might—return to a heterosexual life. Although they are often seen as unreal and untrustworthy, lesbians by choice are ever-present in twentieth-century lesbian communities (Whisman 1994).

As such it is not surprising that the gay men I interviewed were largely unaware that anyone ever identifies as actually choosing to be gay, while the lesbians knew of the pattern, even if they most often disapproved. And most of the women recognized choice as a specifically lesbian experience, while very few of the men did.

> I think there's a division. I think some lesbians are just born to it. And
> some for political reasons. There are certain political reasons that
> yeah, they enjoy sex with men, but politically they really feel that …
> women are much nicer to be around. And then totally divorce them-
> selves from masculine society. (Terry Breiner)

> I think more women would choose than men. And also after getting
> fed up with the male society. I could see that. If I'm a woman, I could
> see that. (Thomas Labadan)

> Lesbians seem to me to choose it more than gay men. I think just in
> terms of politics. I may be wrong, but it seems like women are more,
> that their reasons for being lesbians are sometimes interrelated with
> their politics more than for men. (Karen McNally)

Neither Terry nor Karen felt that they had chosen to be lesbians, and are unusual
among that group for the relatively neutral way they describe those who do.
Negative depictions, such as those above that characterize lesbians by choice as
trendy, man-hating, and confused, were more common.

> Some women have said things like they feel like they have a choice.
> Although I wonder sometimes if people have certain personality
> types where they are more able to deny something that is a real part
> of them, and therefore consider that they have a choice. (Vickie
> Norvell)

Lesbians' and gay men's thinking about chosen homosexuality does not
merely respond to homophobic discourse in a knee-jerk fashion. Concerns
about distinguishing real from false lesbians, for example, reflect the effort to
resist compulsory heterosexuality, not the effort to put forward an acceptable
face. And I do not want to label pro-gay discourse purely reactive, when the
distinction between proactive and reactive rhetoric is artificial at its root. (I
would term the recent right-wing fundamentalist attack a "backlash," to suggest
that *they* are reacting to *us*.) But I do want to point out that all of our thought
and talk about homosexuality takes place in an environment where homosexuality is derivative at best, despicable at worst, and is shaped by that environment
even as it seeks to shape it.

As the next chapter will demonstrate, some of the gay men and lesbians I
interviewed did choose to be gay. Unhindered by the representation of choice as
dangerous, they—along with a few of those who did not choose—talked about
the pleasures of choice. Theirs is an alternative discourse, not often heard and
not always well articulated, in which defending homosexuality is not tied to

repudiating choice. As such, they intervene in the pairing whereby choice is to anti-gay discourse as not-a-choice is to pro-gay discourse.

Pleasures of Choice

Looking over the legislative battle to pass a statewide lesbian and gay rights bill in Massachusetts, activist Masha Gessen regretted pro-gay witnesses' reliance on biological theories of causation, which allowed legislators to hear that "we are victims of nature, pitiable and benign mutants."

> In addition to perpetuating bigoted attitudes outside our community, the claims of having no choice in our sexual orientation exact a great cost on our own community's self-esteem. What backs up those claims are descriptions of gay life as fraught with suffering, as riddled with lies aimed at hiding one's sexuality, as devoid of love and joy (1989: 11).

A handful of the respondents I interviewed voiced similar opinions. Henry Yount, a white man who works as a freelance computer consultant, put it most bluntly.

> I think it's a helpless position to say "I was born this way. It's biological. I can't do anything about it." I think until you see it as something you chose, or choose, you have a weak position.

Relying on the "not a choice" position is "helpless," not empowering or validating.

Even some respondents who felt they did not choose to be gay, and who frowned upon claims that it is possible to do so, implicitly agreed with Henry. They made a rhetorical connection that suggests an intuitive awareness of the heterosexist bias of their position.

> It was never a choice. No. Nor, if your next question is do I regret being gay, the answer is no. (Myron Brown)

> I don't think it's a conscious choice. No, not at all. Not saying that if it was a conscious choice, I wouldn't make it. (Rhia Dill)

Having indicated that they did not choose to be gay/lesbian, Myron and Rhia expect to be asked if they would prefer to be straight. And so they volunteer a disclaimer, telling me (although I did not ask) that having no choice doesn't mean they're dissatisfied with their sexual preference, as though that would logically follow.

When I asked Brian Polaski, a white poet who earns his living as a secretary, if he thought people were born gay he spoke on the topic at length. Like Al Davis, Brian had thought out his position in some detail, but he had come to a radically different conclusion.

> No, I pretty much leave that kind of epistemology ideology up to specialists who have the time to do research on it and write articles on it. It's sort of neither here nor there to me. I don't know; it seems academic. But I lean toward the no. I tend to think that choice is all-important, freedom of choice. I feel less and less sympathetic with psychological theories of causality, even ordinary Freudian ones, that we suffer from our pasts, and are compelled by them. I sort of believe in this possibility of infinite instantaneous liberation from any kind of past, in a moment of absolute choice.

Brian ended his comments by telling a story about being asked to account for his sexuality that identified such a requests as "assaultive," in what was perhaps a subtle evaluation of my question.

> [A group of teenage hoods approached me on a deserted subway platform] and the leader sort of sat down next to me, and was going to intimidate me, and be assaultive by talking to me. And he was going to finally pin me down and make me account for my entire existence, you know, like from the prenatal stage. And he said, "Let me ask you something. Were you born gay, or did you just decide to be that way on your own?" And I looked at him and said, "Were you born stupid, or did you just decide to work at it on your own?"

Brian sees in the heterosexist search for homosexuality's cause a demand that he "account for his entire existence." Refusing to do so, he uses choice to account for his own sexual identity.

Unlike Henry and Brian, Malcolm Wilson, an African-American man who works as an actor and an engineering consultant, says that he did not choose to be gay and believes he may have been born that way. Nonetheless, the notion that homosexuality can be chosen—and that some do choose it—strikes him as empowering, as a sign that "we are not so down by years and years of conditioning." In the story he tells below, other gay men and lesbians respond to a claim of chosen homosexuality in more typical ways.

> [A woman on a panel said she chose to be a lesbian] and the audience was just going crazy! "What does this mean?" And "Well, do you still have an attraction to men?" And she said, "No, I don't." And they

said, "But that can't be, if you had it before." And she said, "Yeah, I used to like cheese but I don't eat cheese any more and I actually don't like it; it was an acquired taste. Men were the acquired taste. I no longer have the taste for them." People were like, "What? Oh, no!" Weeping and gnashing of teeth. But that's interesting. I would like to think that one really has a choice. I would like to think that we are not so down by years and years of conditioning that we can make a choice ourselves.

Luke Hauser, a white man raised on a farm in the Midwest, had just returned from six months in an ashram when we met. His study there brought him to new ways of thinking about choice, even though he had experienced his own coming out as a discovery, not a choice.

In the Hindu tradition, all things are conscious; all things are a choice. We have the power to make those decisions. Part of me feels that's true and part of me doesn't.... I for so long thought that it wasn't a choice, that I was definitely just that. But I think lately I've been feeling that I have the power, if I wanted to, to go the other way. But I also don't see that it's necessary.

As these respondents use it, choice is not the dry and sterile domain of breakfast cereals and consumer products. In these alternative visions, choice is empowering, perhaps even exhilarating. For Brian Polaski, it is the "possibility of infinite instantaneous liberation."

Two distinct views of the individual, and of the source of meaning in life, compete here. Is honor to be found in discovering who and what one is and living true to it, as most of the respondents quoted earlier in this chapter would have it? Or is it to be found in breaking out of such limitations and creating a free self, as Malcolm, Luke, Brian and a few others suggest? These accounts suggest that deliberations about sexual preference bring those who undergo them close to some of the ultimate questions about human existence, in one of the processes that deeply differentiates the experience of marginalized from culturally dominant people.

For the lesbian respondents who present as having chosen their sexual preferences, it was not so much making a choice as making the *right* choice that was liberating. They spoke of their own choices helping them in real ways; unlike the men quoted above, they did not advocate choice in the abstract. These women, many of whom are lesbian-feminists, wish not so much to enter a debate about whether homosexuality is or is not chosen as to claim that lesbianism is a viable option for women.

I was choosing that I didn't want to be with men, and then later I chose that I did want to be with women. I was very excited, I was really happy. And one of the things that tells me it was a big choice for me, was that toward the end of being with that man, I weighed a lot. And I lost like fifteen pounds within the first few months of coming out. Without being on a diet. I just had a feeling it was because I had made a good choice. (Anna Blumberg)

I chose to be happy. I came close. I mean, I was proposed to three times. And each of those guys I really liked. But I wouldn't have been happy with them. Life would've just been mediocre. I could've made it work if I'd wanted to. But I would've never been able to—to feel free. To fly, in life. (Lois Hayes)

This choice, 'cause it really truly has been a choice, it just feels like I made the choice [that's best for me].... And also there's something about being involved this way, like I really feel like I can identify myself as a lesbian, it's very much more powerful than I felt before, as a person. (Diane Rivera)

I was 16 or 17, and I was going to the city to look for the Women's Community.... I was looking for, like, I knew I didn't want to be heterosexual the way it was being presented to me. I was looking for alternatives. (Libby Markowitz)

Thinking about men in terms of all the violence that they commit in our society, and then, do you want to sleep with them? (*Laughs.*) (Pearl Johnson)

Respondents who embraced chosen homosexuality, for themselves or others, inevitably questioned the dichotomous categories of homo- and heterosexuality, agreeing with Kinsey (1948) that "the world is not to be divided into sheep and goats."

I've always thought to myself that surely the most well-adjusted person in the world must be a bisexual who feels comfortable in his or her bisexuality, so that whomever comes along, who attracts you, is someone that you want to be attracted to, and that you're not *bound* to be attracted to one gender or another. (Malcolm Wilson)

A lot of the time I see everyone as gay. I guess, you know, we identify with whatever little kernel of ourselves there is in whomever we see, and most of the time, I respond to the however slight, that gay spark in most people. (Brian Polaski)

As an expected straight child, you're kind of nurtured into all of those situations, where you're kind of helped out all along. (Diane Rivera)

VW: Do you think that most gay men choose to be gay?
PI: Not all of them. I think that part of them choose and part of them grow up that way.
VW: What about heterosexuals?
PI: No, I think that's society. I mean, if there weren't any rules or anything, I think that there'd be a difference. But just because of the way it is, that's the way most people are brought up. (Paul Isaksen)

The discrete categories of homosexual and heterosexual are artificial restraints, according to these statements. Most people have some "gay spark," but being "expected" to be heterosexual they are "brought up" that way and end up straight. But they would be more "well-adjusted" if they were not so limited.

Others linked their critique of the homo/hetero binary more explicitly to choice. They point out that compulsory heterosexuality robs individuals of their ability to choose.

We don't even know what it would be like to choose to be heterosexual, almost, in this society. Because what you've seen on television and in the ads, and on and on, ad infinitum from moment one, and you know, when the first thing ever said about you is "It's a boy" or "It's a girl," you're being shuttled into that traditional gender role. I think it would be nice if change could be made so that all people could be fully human and heterosexuality could be a choice. (Mary Behnke)

I think women have so few choices. Sometimes we think we do, and it's not really a choice. Because I think many, many women are straight because of economics. I think for them marriage is a way of survival. And they may not realize this, but I think it's true. (Virginia Bradford)

I think in a hundred years from now, homosexuals will have provided a means for a healthy heterosexuality. Heterosexuals never make a choice. There is no choice, that's the norm. So it's just as bad for them as it is for homosexuals. Heterosexuals are left in this helpless position also, of "Well, that's the way it is. That's what I'm supposed to do, that's how I'm supposed to behave." And that's not healthy. The route of being attracted to someone because they have the opposite plumbing is just a lie. I'm not heterophobic, but I just look forward to a time when it's a healthy choice, and it's made for good rational reasons, which is that you want to be involved with this person, what-ever their plumbing is. (Henry Yount)

These respondents use the concept of choice to avoid representing homosexuality as a "benign mutation," the social ramifications of which are limited to that minority of individuals who manifest the condition. From this universalizing stance homosexuality is a force for change, "so that all people could be fully human." If heterosexuality is forced on everyone, not merely on those whose homosexual orientation makes it impossible to achieve, then to choose to be gay is to resist coercion, an assertion shared by lesbian-feminist and early gay liberation theory.

> Woman-identified Lesbianism is, then, more than a sexual preference, it is a political choice. It is political because relationships between men and women are essentially political, they involve power and dominance. Since the Lesbian actively *rejects* that relationship and chooses women, she *defies* the established political system. (Bunch 1984, orig. 1975: 144; emphasis added)

> Nature leaves undefined the object of sexual desire. The gender of that object has been imposed socially.... As kids, we *refused to capitulate* to demands that we smother our feeling toward each other. Somewhere we found the strength to *resist* being indoctrinated, and we should count that among our assets. (Wittman 1992, orig. 1970: 331; emphasis added)

The force required to overcome inertia, to resist, can be mustered by choice, according to these statements.

The literal claim that, as the popular lesbian-feminist song had it, "Any woman can...be a lesbian," is easy to discredit as either an accurate description or a practical politics. But that lesbian-feminist idea (along with its lesser known counterpart in gay liberation) asserted that the dichotomous categories of homosexual and heterosexual served the political purpose of maintaining the male-dominant gender order. Gay-positive formulations based upon those dichotomous categories fail to question male dominance.

Most recently, queer theory has taken up the critique of the homo/hetero divide. The literary version uses deconstruction to reveal the hidden workings of the binarism, as Sedgwick (1990) explains:

> [C]ategories presented in a culture as symmetrical binary oppositions—heterosexual/homosexual, in this case—actually subsist in a more unsettled and dynamic tacit relation according to which, first,

term B is not symmetrical with but subordinated to term A; but, second, the ontologically valorized term A actually depends for its meaning on the simultaneous subsumption and exclusion of term B. (10)

The liberatory task, then, is to disrupt the binary construction, to "embrace the indeterminacy of the gay cateogory" (Stein and Plummer 1994; 181), for the category is implicated in our oppression at the same time that it is used by our liberation movements.

It is not necessary to claim that homosexuality is a choice in order to arrive at these insights. It is, in any case, simply untrue that most gay men and lesbians experience their sexual preferences as a conscious choice. But denying the possibility of choice is part of what casts gay-affirmative politics in a narrow mold. A more expansive movement will seek alternatives to compulsory heterosexuality and the gender polarization that is so enmeshed in it (Bem 1993). It will, in Janet Halley's words, "be capacious enough to claim constitutional protection not only for assertions of consolidated and even essentialist gay, lesbian, bisexual, and queer identities, but also for the choice to be queer" (quoted in Minkowitz 1993: 29).

Notes

1. I provide respondents' ages at the time of their interview in late 1987 or early 1988.

2. In 1987, Al Davis is enthusiastic about evidence that homosexuality may be biological. He and others like him already form a receptive audience for the bio-research announcements of 1991 and succeeding years.

3. Exactly the same reasoning appears in the characterization of pediatric and hemophiliac people with AIDS as "innocent," marking homosexual men and IV drug users as "guilty."

three

Stories of Choice

I began this research intending to compare choosers and non-choosers, and I kept a two-by-two table ("Gender: Male/Female" by "Account: Choice/Non-choice") on my wall, which I planned to fill with names as I conducted my interviews. But I had a terrible time figuring out where people fit; I would place a name in the "Choice" column one day, and move it over to the "Non-choice" column the next. Gay and lesbian accounts of choice, I eventually admitted, cannot be so neatly dichotomized. A more accurate typology describes three approaches to the role of choice:[1] Most respondents claim both choice and non-choice, by carefully distinguishing what can and cannot be chosen—roughly, "doing" and "being." Those who do not make such a distinction feel either that they had exercised no choice at all, or that they had fully chosen their sexual identities. As they explain their experiences and their accounts, they theorize the relationships between such concepts as essence and existence, choice and determination, sexual preference and sexual orientation.[2]

Accounts of Determination

Four women and five men consistently report that they exercised no choice at all, both in response to the direct questions and in the context of the entire interview. They rely on a determinist model to account for their homosexuality. Sandie and William tell their stories using themes that are repeated often by this group of respondents: early awareness of homoerotic feelings, gender nonconformity, and a relatively unconflicted transition into an active gay life—and most notably for the purposes of the typology I am developing here, Sandie, William, and the others of this group recall no decisions, choices, or deliberations in the making of that transition.

Sandie Martin is a 29-year-old white woman who works as an insurance underwriter and lives in Brooklyn with her lover of eight years. She was born the youngest of five children to a working-class family in New Jersey that became poor when Sandie's father left them six years later. She did not finish high school, but later completed her GED and earned a degree from a local community college. Sandie feels that she's always been gay, and is unable to pinpoint a time when she came out.

> Yeah, I've been a tomboy from day one. Never attracted to men, never saw anything in men. It's like it was something that's always been. I never sat down and said, "Well, I'm gay now." It's just I've always been. Always attracted to girls when I was a kid, in high school, and I never really had a hard time trying to find out if I was straight or if I was gay. I just stayed gay.

Her first sexual relationship was with another girl when both were fourteen years old.

> SM: I had a relationship with a woman, a girl I was going to school with. We grew up together, so I don't know if it was a relationship or if it was just something that happened between us. It never happened again. It was only the one time.
> VW: So what did you think right after that?
> SM: I said, "This is it!" (We *both laugh*.) "It couldn't be any better than this."

In spite of her awareness of her sexual preference, she went on to have boyfriends in high school. But she knew that she had no real interest in them.

> I was different. Because I didn't feel that same way the other girls felt. I didn't drool over the boys; I didn't talk about the hunks. The girls, they all had boyfriends. "Why doesn't Sandie have a boyfriend? What's wrong with Sandie?" Peer pressure. More than that I felt this was something I had to do.

She hung out with a crowd of gay kids, sometimes going to the local bars with them when they could get in. She rarely regretted being a lesbian, but she knew it was going to make her life harder.

There were times when I felt I was hurting my mom, I was hurting my family, I was hurting myself. Because I knew it wasn't gonna be easy. You know, I had some times when I was wondering if it was the right thing I was doing. But basically for other people's worries more than myself. I knew it was right for me but I didn't think it was right for them.

She is quite certain that no part of her lesbianism was a choice.

I don't think I had a choice in this. It's just something I was steered toward since day one. I've sat down and talked to my brothers, and my brothers have said that they knew something was wrong when I was a child. Something was different about me. It's just the way I've always been; I never thought about being any other way.

William Sloan, the oldest of my respondents, is a 63-year-old retired school-teacher who holds a master's degree. He was born to a white working-class family in New York City, and his father died soon after, leaving William's mother with eight children to raise alone in the Depression. Like Sandie, he always knew he was gay.

I have been gay all my life. I had no real coming out because I can distinctly remember having gay imagery, gay thoughts, that I can now see were gay, as early as five. There was never any doubt in my mind as to what I was interested in, so none of the usual anxieties and crises, and so on, that I read about and hear about from other gay and lesbian people. It was a fact: Psychologically or emotionally or whatever you want to call it, I was always attracted to males. Even when I was ten or eleven I was already strongly attracted to men, and already looking at them. When I was unhappy at home, I had this future vision that I could look toward of finding some man with whom I could go off and share an apartment. I wasn't even thinking overtly that much about sex, as just life together with another young man. Two handsome young bachelors about town, in one studio, I would think. And I had that ongoing from about ten years on.

He remembers as a young teenager thinking of himself as gay—the term he preferred to homosexual—and this identification preceded his first sexual experience at age seventeen. Before that, he was befriended by an adult gay man who validated his identity in terms that were unspoken but understood.

He was extremely handsome. Very nice, very intelligent, very patient. And I used to sit and talk to him, and we never discussed the problems of being gay. He took it for granted after one or two conversations, he took it for granted, not only that I was going to be gay but that I knew I was going to be gay and that there were no conflicts. And we never talked about that. We talked about the arts and the humanities.

He dated a woman for a brief time after high school, but felt it was a farce—"After I would go out with her, I would leave her and I would go to a gay bar"—and soon broke it off. Like Sandie, he is certain that his homosexuality was never a choice.

My choice was made for me the day I began. I never had the slightest feeling of choice. It was so in me that my conflicts were never with being gay. My conflicts were mainly concerned with getting control of my life, away from my family.

All of the respondents in this group concur with Sandie and William in their accounts of the extent to which they chose their homosexuality. This account is characterized by a complete lack of choice, and I call it the "determined" account.

For me it was never a choice. For me it was the only way to be. (Justine DiAngelo)

Well, I was just always—I never thought of myself as straight. I never thought of myself as anything but lesbian, and so it was never a question. I mean I never went out with boys. (Terry Breiner)

These respondents experience who they are, what they feel, and what they do as one seamless reality. In effect, they do not distinguish between their sexual orientation and their sexual preference.

My use of the terms "sexual preference" and "sexual orientation" does not so much enter as sidestep the debate about which is the better term, for I do not take them as synonyms. A sexual preference is a pattern of sexual/affectional desires of which the individual is aware, much like any other form of preference or taste. A sexual orientation, on the other hand, is an internal condition which may be latent or unknown. As such, the relationship between the two terms is not so much competitive as theoretical: A sexual preference may or may not always be the causal outcome of a sexual orientation. In a gender-polarized society, most people have a sexual preference for either men or women. Whether or not all individuals have a sexual orientation toward one or the other is more difficult to determine (as is the question of whether or not orientations even exist independently of social factors—cross-culturally and trans-historically).

Mixed Accounts

The largest group of respondents, 23 women and 22 men, combined elements of choice and determination in their accounts. It was not a quantitative mix ("a little chosen, a little determined"), but a qualitative one. Respondents distinguished quite clearly between those aspects of their sexualities that were and were not chosen, differentiating being and doing, essence and existence. The respondents described below, like the others who use the "mixed" account, vary as to whether they always knew they were gay. They also came out at a wide range of ages, and after diverse sexual histories. Some grew up typically gendered for their class, race, and region, while others were gender nonconformists.

My first interview was with Robert Henderson, a 33-year-old white man who was working as an administrative assistant to an antique dealer. He was the first of three children born to a middle-class, Southern Baptist couple in a small Texas city. After two years at a state university, Robert moved to New York. He was not always aware of his homosexuality, but he does remember some early homoerotic feelings, and recalls that he was "not at all boyish." He discovered (or rediscovered) his attraction to men at age eighteen, and was shocked by it.

> [At a summer job after high school] there were openly gay men who came on to me. And just put me off the deep end for some reason. I mean, I went into a real trauma shock at these people coming on to me. And so I had a cousin who's gay who was around at the time, and he kind of said, "Well, it's okay, you know. Just because this person did a number on you doesn't mean you have to get blown out of shape if you don't want to be. And if you're not gay, that's fine. But if you are, then that's something for you to think about." And I said, "Oh, maybe I am! You know, after all these years, maybe that's what all those things meant." It was all the pieces falling into place after a lot of confusion, especially after a lot of adolescent experimentation with my friends, that for some reason completely zipped out of my mind for a few years in high school when I dated girls.

Robert had not dated girls in high school to cover up his homosexuality; he was genuinely interested in them, and one relationship lasted a year-and-a-half.

> VW: Did you think at the time that you loved her?
> RH: I think so, yeah. Definitely. I was very sincere, and I don't think I was going along with it just to go along with it, although now that's what I think I was doing. I think I was sincere in that I liked her a lot and I felt a lot of things for her, and as an adolescent I did have a lot of sexual desires, which I probably projected onto her and felt for her in some ways.

After "all the pieces fell into place" at age eighteen, Robert never again felt attracted to women. He is certain that he would have discovered his homosexuality eventually.

> VW: Have you ever thought about what would have happened if your cousin hadn't sort of taken you under his wing and talked to you? I mean, have you ever thought that you'd still be living as a straight person?
>
> RH: Oh no, no, no. No way. I know myself well enough to know that it would have been a matter of "until the right person came on to me." These people that were in their thirties were coming on to me when I was eighteen, and I wasn't attracted to them. But it would've been just a matter of the right person coming into my life who made me realize it. I was overdue for pulling all that together anyway.

When I asked him about the role of choice in becoming gay, he distinguished carefully what was and was not chosen.

> I think it's a conscious choice to be open, and to be positive about it, and to try to live my life the best way I can, but as far as the choice between heterosexuality and homo, I don't think there ever was a choice for me. At least if there was, it was before I was two or three years old....The lifestyle may be a choice, but not the actual desire.

Claire Williams is a 23-year-old black woman who writes for local lesbian and gay publications and works as an administrative assistant for an AIDS service organization. She was the third of four children in a middle-class Queens family. She completed a year of college immediately after high school, and plans to finish her degree someday. Claire remembers feeling different as a child, but because she was one of only a few African-Americans in a mostly white school, not because of her sexuality or gender (she was not a tomboy). Like Robert, she was not continuously aware of her homosexuality. She remembers some erotic feelings for women in her teen years, including crushes on teachers, which she did not then understand.

> I didn't have any understanding of that; I didn't have a label for what I was feeling. I had an unbelievable, passionate crush on Lindsay Wagner, the Bionic Woman? It made no sense. I just knew I died to watch this show. The show came out in the early seventies, so I guess I was a preteen. She had this little scar on her lip, and I always had images of putting my mouth on that scar, which is on a woman's lip. And I didn't think, "Oh, no, what does this mean?"

Claire had boyfriends, including a serious relationship in her senior year of high school. But she could not bring herself to have sex with him.

> I tried and it was painful. It just wasn't going to work. There was no way I was going to relax into this or whatever. But I really cared about this guy.

Claire was troubled by this, and sought out the help of a slightly older friend. The desires she found herself feeling for that woman helped trigger her self-discovery.

> I was talking to her about it, and at some point I just felt this overwhelming desire to kiss her. [Later that year, writing in my journal] I needed to find out what this was, not just about women but about Charles, about men and boys. I wrote constantly, and I wrote what I call my coming out story, where I talked about [all my memories of homoerotic feelings]. I had to pursue this.

Like Robert, Claire's "mixed" account distinguishes the chosen and determined parts of her lesbianism.

> It wasn't a choice I made. I don't feel I had a choice in the matter. I choose to be a political lesbian; I choose to be an out lesbian. I don't think I chose to be a lesbian. I think I could've been a lesbian whether or not I fooled around with men. Whether or not I got married, or whatever one does. I think I still would've been a lesbian.

Paula Weiss is a 25-year-old Jewish white woman, who has been waiting tables since she left college after two years. Paula was the youngest of two children born to a middle-class Manhattan couple, and was never a tomboy. Unlike Claire and Robert, she was continuously aware of her sexual feelings for women.

> I told my mother I first had feelings toward women when I was fourteen. It was there always. I just remember being very attracted to a camp counselor, and girlfriends of my brother. You know I was eight and his girlfriends would be fourteen or fifteen and I knew I just wanted to be around them and I recognized it as a sexual thing. I knew. I always read a lot and I knew the word early on, and I think originally I thought I was bisexual.

Throughout her teenage years, she shifted back and forth between bisexual and lesbian identities.

It wasn't being with a woman that scared me; it was the not being with men. I think at one point when I was sixteen, I walked into my shrink's office and said, "Listen, I'm not bisexual. I'm definitely gay." I had gone to see Melissa Manchester, and I shook her hand and I thought, "Wow, a woman's hand is so different. Who am I kidding?" And it really hit me very hard. And then, again I would turn back to the bisexual thing.

After several years of sexual experiences with both men and women, Paula recently decided to identify exclusively as a lesbian.

I never thought that I was bisexual from anything in here [*touching her chest*], inside me. I always thought it here [*pointing to her head*], that I had to be bisexual. I never felt sexually attracted to men. I would want to be with them sexually just because then I would feel like a "real woman." But when I was in bed, I would feel like, "What am I doing here?" I finally got fed up with just trying to sleep with men all the time and not feeling anything, and I realized it was crazy. So that's really when I said, "I'm gay." I had to keep telling myself.

Paula, too, offers the "mixed" account: She chose her behavior, but not her desires.

The feelings that I feel toward women certainly aren't a choice. It's my choice to pursue relationships, emotional and sexual relation-ships; that part is a choice. But I don't think the feelings are a choice.

Thomas Labadan, a 27-year-old man born in the Philippines, immigrated to the U.S. twelve years ago, accompanied by his six older siblings and his parents, who took service jobs in New York despite their higher levels of education and experience. Thomas has a bachelor's degree in music, and works as a clerk in an accounting firm. Like Paula, Thomas was always aware of his homoerotic feelings.

I had an attraction toward the same sex since, I couldn't remember when. At the age of eight? Or seven. When I, you know, started devel-oping sexual desires it was geared towards men, certainly not with girls.

Thomas's male relatives ridiculed him for playing with dolls, calling him "that sissy." He remembers comparing himself to an effeminate gay man in his Manila neighborhood.

TL: I would hear stories about, like, "the faggot of the block." All the boys would go in and get free haircuts from him, in exchange for, well, you know. One day when I was eight or nine he told me, "Oh, do you still play with dolls? Come down and I'll teach you something." My brother was, "No, no, no. Don't do that to him." Although my brothers were protective of me, they were doing it. They were having sex with this guy, the faggot of the block. It's fine to have sex with men as long as the roles are played.

VW: You were seeing how the straight men treated this guy, like "the faggot of the block." So that was something you wanted to avoid for yourself?

TL: No, no, no. I wished I could do what he was doing, but I didn't do anything till later.

He was uncomfortable with his sexual feelings, and for a while planned to become a priest. He thought moving to the U.S. would change him, and when it didn't, he contacted a gay-youth group. When he left home to go to college a couple of years later, he tried dating women for a short time. Then his developing gay identity blossomed.

There was a period there when I would say maybe I was bisexual. That's a very short period, I'll tell you that. (*Laughs.*) It was a period I didn't want to label myself, the first month at college. And then after that I met my lover and said, "I'm not bisexual." (*We laugh.*)

His account mixes elements of choice and determinism.

It's not something that is a decision. I decide to live, to lead a gay lifestyle. But I had an attraction to the same sex since I was, I couldn't remember when.... It's the lifestyle I chose.

In their use of the "mixed" account, respondents made many distinctions between what they did and did not choose. Several said their actual sexual behavior was chosen, but the desire behind it was not:

In terms of choosing, like I said, I went out to the clubs on my own. Nobody forced me. I wanted to experiment with a woman, you know. And, you know, I'm glad I did. (Jessica Padilla)

Well, I was very conscious when I made the choice to choose a woman to sleep with, but I don't know what it had to do with it, because I don't think I could feel good and have a relationship with a man. (Patty Irving)

I believe that being homosexual is something that I did not choose, necessarily, to be. My choice is to act on it. Um, because I can't remember a time when I wasn't having homosexual thoughts. (Dwight Russell)

It's been a conscious choice of living it. You know, of taking a step and saying, "Yes, I'm going to be with men." Um, but I don't think there's a conscious choice at all, I didn't turn around one day and say "Hey, I'm not going to like women anymore." I never did, you know, in a sexual way. (Jack Miklowicz)

I don't believe it's a matter of choice. The only choice you have is to act on your sexuality. Choose to act on it or not act on it. But to choose your sexuality is [impossible]. (Sam Broome)

Some of the women in this group specifically mention choosing to stop dating or having sex with men, while no men specifically mention making a decision to stop seeing women. (This choice, to cease involvement with men, is also mentioned by women who claim to have chosen much more, who will be discussed below.)

I decided, no more men in my life. Absolutely. At 21, no more men. (Mara Pettinelli)

I felt all of the sudden more positive and good about my experiences with women, so I made a decision, you know, not to be bothered with men anymore. (Vickie Norvell)

Some respondents indicated that, while their underlying homosexuality was not chosen, seeing themselves as homosexual, adopting a personal identity as a gay man or lesbian, was a choice. They could have chosen to deny or ignore their sexual feelings, but they would still have been homosexual.

In a way it could be a conscious choice, just to acknowledge it within yourself, so that's kind of like saying that you are a lesbian. (Cindy Schwartz)

You know when people talk about it being a choice, I really don't. I mean I feel like I did make the choice to discover who I am, but I didn't at all make the choice to be gay. (Sharon Halpern)

No, I don't think it was a choice. But I could choose to allow this part of myself to be expressed, or I could hide that part of myself forever. But it definitely was inside of me. (Sherry Pero)

When you talk about choice, to me it means choice of accepting who you are, and living that life. Maybe that's the better response for me, to choosing, than whether it's men or women, or heterosexual or homosexual. (Sol Davidoff)

Yes, it's a conscious decision not to deny it. (Ralph Myers)

In addition to one's personal identity, one has a public identity, the label by which one is known by friends, family, the world at large. Some respondents mentioned choosing to make these match. They chose to be out, but not to be gay.

It's really the choice of acceptance of who I am and being proud of that, of being out and being comfortable. I'm pretty out, so that's good. The choice of being a lesbian, there's no choice in that, it's a fact. (Katie Lee)

My own experience, the feelings were totally unwelcome when they first came along. So sexuality may be biological, or whatever. But all identity is political, and that's something I've clearly chosen. (Maurice Raymond)

I've been gay ever since I've known me. I think deciding to be out about it is a choice. But, I guess I'm not a big believer in the "gay is a choice" theory. (Al Davis)

Finally, some respondents mention choosing to lead a gay/lesbian lifestyle. Although the term "lifestyle" has been used pejoratively in homophobic discourse, these respondents use it descriptively. Here, it is a loosely defined concept which contains elements of all three concepts given above—sexual behavior, personal identity, and public identity—plus behavior that is not specifically sexual or intimate, such as attending lesbian/gay cultural events, belonging to lesbian/gay friendship circles, or frequenting lesbian/gay bars.

I don't feel like I had a choice, because sometimes if I had had a choice, I would probably have chosen to be straight. It would be a lot simpler being straight. You know, so making a choice to be a lesbian sometimes doesn't seem right. However, by choice, I live a lesbian lifestyle. Like my close friends are all women, the people I go to for advice are women, everybody around me are women. (Lucinda Alomar)

I guess if I really forced myself, I could live a heterosexual lifestyle. In most cases, I can pass as heterosexual. The choice is to be either a), repressed, b), in the closet, or c), to be who and what I am. (Vivienne Medina)

A gay lifestyle I think is a conscious choice. Being gay itself is not a choice. (Billy Fine)

To me it feels like I'm actually making a conscious choice only when I'm doing something that most people consider gay. Like going to a gay bar, or going to a gay event. (Darren Walker)

The "mixed" account distinguishes between sexual orientation and sexual preference by claiming that the former is determined and the latter is chosen. The two realms are not only separate, but ontologically different: A homosexual orientation is a positive reality whether or not it is acted upon, accepted, or even known. Almost all of the respondents who used the "mixed" account believe it is possible to be homosexual without knowing it, although most think one would discover it eventually. They believe that they either were born homosexual or became so at an early age, although for many, the distinction doesn't matter. Their inclusion of elements of choice in their accounts does not disturb their determinist and positivist understanding of sexual *orientation*.

But self-knowledge is entirely implicated in sexual *preference*: If one accepts, recognizes, acts upon, and integrates knowledge of one's homosexual orientation, then and only then does one manifest a homosexual preference. At various times in their pasts, many of these respondents had heterosexual and bisexual preferences. But, they maintain, their true orientation was always homosexual. A preference is subject to choice and change; an orientation is not.

The Rejection of Absolute Choice

In the quotations above, respondents of the Determined and Mixed groups discuss the aspects of their lives they feel can be chosen: actual sexual behavior, public and private identity, lifestyle. In this section, they delineate what cannot be chosen. The wording of my question, "To what extent do you feel that being lesbian/gay is a conscious choice that you have made?" encourages respondents to clarify the limits of choice, not the limits of determinism. So most respondents who offered the "determined" and "mixed" accounts provide some argument, usually without further prompting, for their claim that they did not choose their sexual orientations.

Some invoke physical sensation or intuition, making a claim that their underlying homosexuality just didn't feel chosen.

> If homosexuality is not innate, it feels that way. It was no choice what-
> ever as far as the basic impulse goes. My earliest attractions were to
> men. The choice I made was to ignore it and say I wanted to be het-
> erosexual, but it wasn't a choice I had it in me to make. It was like
> choosing to be green, or choosing to be a bird. It was not a viable
> choice. When I moved into the gay community, it was relaxing, just
> letting myself be. (Morton Phelps, Mixed)

> VW: To what extent do you feel being a lesbian has been a con-
> scious choice?
> RB: Well, not to a great extent. Because it's pretty inherent. So the
> conscious choice would've had to have been made to be straight.
> But this was more natural. (Rhonda Barker, Determined)

> I don't think it's a conscious choice. No, not at all. It's more from the
> inside than the outside. With that, I think I do things more from feel-
> ing than actually thinking about it. I do think a lot; I think about every-
> thing. But I think [being a lesbian] has a lot of feeling, not something
> that you choose. (Rhia Dill, Mixed)

> It was almost a matter of being a physical thing. I don't see how it could
> be biological but it almost feels that way. (Celia Daugherty, Mixed)

Other respondents present some sort of evidence to support their claims that
they did not choose their sexual orientation. For some, the evidence is their own
self-knowledge; they always knew about their homosexuality. If they never had
any other options, then they could never have made a choice.

> If it's a choice at all, I think that's still kind of a hotly debated thing. I
> don't know, but I can only reiterate by saying that I've always known.
> (Eric Lehman, Mixed)

> I've been gay ever since I've known me. (Al Davis, Mixed)

> It's just the way I've always been; I never thought about being any
> other way. (Sandie Martin, Determined)

Others refer to their early experiences with desire, attraction, and fantasy. For
these respondents, timing is key: If homoerotic feelings appeared before the

respondent was old enough to seek them out, or even to know what they were, then the respondent could not have chosen her/his sexual orientation:

> My own experience, the feelings were totally unwelcome when they first came along [at age 13]. So sexuality may be biological, or whatever. (Maurice Raymond, Mixed)

> It was no choice whatever as far as the basic impulse goes. My earliest attractions were to men. (Morton Phelps, Mixed)

> I don't [think it was a choice], you know, since I was initially attracted to women. I mean, do you really choose what your taste is? (Barbara Linders, Mixed)

And a few even provide some outside corroboration:

> I think I've been gay from birth. Those two experiences [where others called me "sissy"] sort of corroborate that, because even before I knew anything about sexuality or anything about conditioning or anything, I was obviously exhibiting gay behavior. (Malcolm Wilson, Determined)

> For me it was never a choice.... My mother swears up and down she knew even before I did I was going to be gay. She won't tell me how she knows; she just knows that she knows. (Justine DiAngelo, Determined)

The quotations above are examples of the sort of evidence some respondents used to indicate that their homosexual orientation is an essential, unchosen part of who they are. Respondents also provided evidence to demonstrate that they are not, and could not be, heterosexual.

> I don't think there's a conscious choice at all; I didn't turn around one day and say, "Hey, I'm not going to like women anymore." I never did, you know, in a sexual way. (Jack Miklowicz, Mixed)

> It was no choice at all as far as the basic impulse goes.... I've always been attracted to men. I've never felt more than a twinge or two for women. (Morton Phelps, Mixed)

> I went out with guys, right? I chose to go out with guys. But you know, there was something missing there. The sexual needs. I didn't feel exactly the same way I felt when I was a with a woman. Plain and simple. With men there was always something missing. (Jessica Padilla, Mixed)

I don't really know if it's a choice for me. Because I sure tried to be bisexual. And I couldn't be bisexual. I don't feel like I had a choice, because sometimes if I had had a choice, I would probably have chosen to be straight. (Lucinda Alomar, Mixed)

Although several respondents agree with Lucinda that, at some point in the past, they would have chosen heterosexuality if they could, only two respondents argue that they have no choice by stating that if a choice were available, they would even now choose to be straight. John's statement is the stronger of the two:

I don't like saying I'm gay because I really don't want to be gay. If I had a choice, I wish I was heterosexual. To me being gay is only a weak— it's not a weakness as much as it is something that is not accepted by society and it is not making my life any easier. It doesn't make me feel any better about myself. (John Chambers, Mixed)

These arguments demonstrate the essentialist and determinist nature of most respondents' conceptions of homosexuality. Their sexual preference is part of who they are. Therefore, for some, knowledge of it is as subjective and intuitive as knowledge of one's body—they know it's there because they can feel it. As with other essential features of the individual, homosexuality is seen as unchanging and consistent throughout the life course. Thus, if homosexuality was present at an early age, it cannot have been chosen at a later age. Homosexuality is a condition. It is more than the sum of the fantasies, attractions, and feelings that are offered as indicators of an underlying orientation.[3]

The essentialist perspective characterizes homosexuality and heterosexuality as polar opposites. They are both conceived as sexual orientations, as positive and negative images of each other. Therefore, respondents reason that choice implies choosing between them, possible only where homosexual and heterosexual feelings are experienced as equivalent options. (As the writings of the emerging bisexual movement argue, bisexuality is frequently defined in similar terms, as qualitatively and quantitatively equal sexual feelings for men and women, a definition that fuels the argument that bisexuality doesn't really exist. See Hutchins and Kaahumanu, 1991).

Two women from the "mixed" account are less certain than the others that they reject the concept of choice. In spite of the fact that both have stated that they did not choose to be lesbian, but only to act on it, Jessica and Lucinda flirt here with the idea that they may have chosen more than that. But in the end, both of them back away from claiming that they chose to be lesbians.

JP: [My mother] says, "You were not born like this. This is what you chose. So, hey, this is the consequences, you know. You could've been with a guy." And blah, blah, blah, the whole bit.

VW: Do you think that's true?

JP: Maybe if my life would've been different? Like wow, I would've been happy [*ironically*]. Happy with what? He's gonna be the breadwinner, the whole typical thing, you know. But I wasn't gonna let myself be fooled. Maybe there was an influence, maybe because I saw the way that my father treated my mother. Subconsciously, that I grew up looking at this, you know? And okay, but I still felt the sexual feelings that I did. Because we're talking about something different now, in terms of sexual preference, from what I saw with her. (Jessica Padilla, Mixed)

Lucinda felt emotionally but not sexually drawn to women from an early age and, after some years of trying to relate to men, made a decision to round out her attraction to women by developing her sexual desire for them. In the passage below, she reflects on this complex process of choice.

When you try to pass a gay-rights bill there's a lot of discussion within the gay movement, there used to be, whether you would put "sexual orientation" or "sexual preference." One means you chose it, the other means you were born that way. I myself don't feel I had a choice, but in some ways, some ways, like in choosing to try to become sexually attracted to women when I wasn't, I chose that. I could have said, "Well, I can't be attracted to women, let me just drop it." Yet I did try to choose to be bisexual and it didn't happen. This is very confusing. I haven't resolved these two things yet. I don't know, I don't even think it's necessary for me to figure it out. (Lucinda Alomar, Mixed)

Those who claim a "chosen" account say what, in the end, Jessica and Lucinda do not—that the choices one makes about doing impact one's being, so one can choose to be gay.

Chosen Accounts

The third group (six men and twelve women) indicated that they chose more than "doing," that they had in some way chosen what those above would distinguish as "being," and they clearly saw themselves as a minority. "Chosen" accounts vary much more than either "determined" or "mixed accounts," and are grouped together here as much by the convention I have adopted as by internal coherence. There are three subtypes of the "chosen" account: the bisexual account, used by both men and women; the feminist account, used solely by women; and idiosyncratic accounts, offered here only by men. (I anticipated that men who use any form of "chosen" account would be difficult to locate, and I was not disappointed. Unfortunately I ended up with only six of them, so my observations of this group are tentative.)

Diane Rivera offers a well-articulated bisexual account. She is a 23-year-old Latina artist who was born in Los Angeles to a working-class couple who split up after Diane's two younger sisters were born. She moved out on her own before she finished high school, and completed a year of college while working a number of jobs. Currently, she studies painting and works part-time as an office temp. Diane believes she was raised to be bisexual: Her mother, although heterosexual, had many gay and lesbian friends, and encouraged Diane to choose her own sexuality.

> I really, truly believe that the way I was brought up with my mother was that basically you fall in love with, you have sexual things with, and you bond with whoever. I guess I can still say it really has to do with the person, and all that garbage. I feel that, you know, as a base.

Although she had intense relationships with her female friends, Diane's first sexual and emotional relationships were with men, including Neil, with whom she lived for two years. Soon after they got together, Diane began to feel more attracted to women. Neil encouraged her to explore those feelings, yet was jealous as well. She became involved with another woman who was also living with a man.

> We were in a very experimental stage together, figuring out what we liked. She had a boyfriend, and another girlfriend, so I feel like I chose a very safe situation to be involved with a woman.

When the relationship with Neil ended, she began to think of herself as a lesbian, and to have more casual relationships with women.

> Then things started to really change, and it was a really, really wonderful year. I lived alone, and I stayed out of really messy relationships, and I started to develop more bonds to lesbian friends that I had, and um, more identify myself with the community. So in very small ways, I started reading books, going to gay bookstores; that was the only way I knew to really identify myself without—, I was really afraid to get involved in a relationship. I ended up having small things here and there, the old girlfriend of this girlfriend of your best friend's neighbor's gay lover, you know.

No one around Diane was surprised or upset when she began identifying as a lesbian.

> It wasn't very hard for me to tell my mother, or tell my stepfather. My mother was just kind of, "Oh, well, I was waiting for this." And my stepfather was amazingly supportive. And my friends were like, "Oh, that's really neat, Diane, let's meet this new girl."

She's quite certain that her lesbianism is chosen.

> I guess I never felt that it wasn't a choice. It was an option, I guess. There was certainly a time when I pretty much could have allowed myself to kind of float along, and kind of claim a bisexual lifestyle. But afterwhile I thought, "I think for me that's just playing it a little safe." Because I didn't want to continue to keep men in my life. This choice, cause it really truly has been a choice, it just feels much more powerful than I felt before, as a person.... I don't think that I don't like having sex with men, 'cause I do, but all the things I love about relating to people sexually just have a whole different feel, way more deeper, with women.

Diane is well aware of how different her account is from the other lesbians she knows, and that troubles her.

> I wish I was one of these, "I knew when I was in high school, I knew when I was in little baby school." Sometimes I feel like if I was younger, and dealt with it in a younger way, maybe it would be easier for me now. Seems like it would have been a lightbulb going off.

Art Turner is a 44-year-old insurance salesman with a college degree who lives with his lover of seventeen years. Art is the only child of a working-class white couple in Indianapolis, but unlike Diane, was not raised to be bisexual. He was not a "sissy boy," had girlfriends in high school, and married when he was twenty-four. The year before, he had experienced his first sexual encounter with a man, but he did not come away from it thinking of himself as gay.

> In 1967 I met somebody in New York in Times Square, which is not the place to meet someone. That was my first sexual experience, with a man, but I still didn't identify myself. I guess I found it enjoyable, but it was something that you do for amusement, entertainment in Sin City, particularly in Sin City in Times Square, what more do you want? (Laughs.) So that was in sixty-seven. Sixty-eight I got married.... Prior to getting married, I did have that experience in New York. I guess I kind of wondered about that, but I thought I was in love with her, and I was. And I was from Indianapolis; I didn't know gay life existed.

The marriage lasted only two years, ending when his wife left him and moved back back in with her parents. Art's interest in men, of which his wife never knew, was not the cause of the breakup. But when the marriage ended, he began thinking about his sexuality.

> The divorce was the turning point of my identity. At that point, I
> started remembering what had happened before. The next summer I
> passed through Chicago and decided to spend the night there. That's
> where I had my next experience.

After that trip, he found the gay bars of Indianapolis, "and that became a wild
summer." The next year he moved to New York and settled into Greenwich
Villege, where he "lived in a completely gay world." During that time he looked
back over his life and recognized signs that he had been interested in men long
before he had realized it.

> Going back into high school, I would look at some of my classmates
> but I didn't know what was going on, why I was so interested in, "Oh,
> he's good-looking; oh, he's a good athlete; oh, he's smart; oh, he's
> whatever." Between college and getting married I had that one expe-
> rience in New York, but I guess I didn't know there was a life you
> could live. Maybe there was an attraction to it, but it's like going to an
> amusement park. I go to Disneyland. I *love* going to Disneyland, but
> that's not a life. That's probably how I thought about it.

Art identifies strongly as a gay man, but believes that his underlying orientation
is bisexual.

> I sort of feel that there's a continuum, and I'm on the continuum. I really
> wonder what my life would be like if my marriage had worked out and
> we would have eventually had kids. My gut level feeling would be that
> some time in my life, later on, I would end up in a situation that proba-
> bly would have rekindled things. Now I'm living in a gay environment,
> do I ever look over in the other direction? If my relationship ended
> now, I can tell you, I couldn't get back into the bar scene if my life
> depended on it. Say in the interim, I would meet a woman that I like, I
> don't know what would happen, I really don't. But I think that's unlikely
> because this is my world. I don't know that many straight people.

When he looks back on his life now, he sees his homosexuality as chosen.

> VW: To what extent do you think that being gay is a conscious
>   choice that you've made?
> AT: There's a poem by Robert Frost that's called "The Road Not
>   Taken," and it ends something like, "I took the road less trav-
>   eled by and that has made all the difference," or something like
>   that, and really, my whole life has been that way. I have always

considered that, just because everybody else was doing something, that didn't mean I would do it. And when I think about it,
being gay is that way, too.

Art is one of three men who feel that their true sexual orientation is bisexual;
they chose to develop their feelings for men and eventually extinguish their feelings
for women. They made these decisions gradually, over a number of years. Rick
Gross, a 38-year-old Jewish man from the Bronx, who is a freelance writer, explains:

> I think I am bisexual. Most of my experience is with men, but I enjoy
> having sex with women. I went through this particularly frustrating
> period that when I was in bed with a man, I wished it was a woman,
> and when I was in bed with a woman, I would wish that it was a man.
> And if people asked me, I would say I was gay, because saying you're
> bisexual sounds like such bullshit most of the time. I feel my life could
> have gone in different directions. But it wasn't a choice as if I sat down
> at the table and arranged my papers and sort of made a checklist.

Four women, like these men, framed their "chosen" account in terms of
bisexuality.

> Yes, it's a choice. We're all basically bisexual; I could love a man if I
> wanted to, but I like to prefer women. (Leah Rosenthal)

> VW: Do you feel like you chose to be a lesbian?
> TF: Yeah.
> VW: Could you have chosen not to be?
> TF: I could have, but I also felt that if I didn't like it, that I could
>   always walk away from it. I didn't feel that it was anything I had
>   to commit myself to. 'Cause I, you know, I just didn't feel that
>   way.... But I *don't* think that you can love two people, each of
>   the opposite sex, at the same time. (Tina Fiore)

Implicitly, those who offer the bisexual version of the "chosen" account distinguish between orientation and preference. As they see it, they have been able
to choose a homosexual preference precisely because they have an underlying
bisexual orientation. As one put it, "I'm technically bisexual." But unlike those
who feel that they have a homosexual orientation, they do not see themselves as
essentially different from heterosexuals, and they question the assumptions that
everyone is either gay or straight, and that most people are inherently straight.
Rather, they see heterosexuality as a sort of programmed default, and believe
that many more people would be bisexual if they questioned that.

How many straight people, if there weren't the cultural taboos, would be a little more bisexual? (Art Turner)

I always wonder, how many women kind of lead their regular heterosexual lives, but really don't feel like that? Cause there's not a real distinct place to go with it? You kind of have to jut yourself out, and it's a big risk. Just because of where it sits in society, I think it just takes either some kind of frantic place where you can't deal with not dealing with it, or you just really choose it. (Diane Rivera)

VW: Do you think that most gay men choose to be gay?
PI: Not all of them. I think that part of them choose and part of them grow up that way.
VW: What about heterosexuals?
PI: No, I think that's society. I mean, if there weren't any rules or anything, I think that there'd be a difference. But just because of the way it is, that's the way most people are brought up. (Paul Isaksen)

A lot of people are so lonely, they're unhappy; they say; "I need someone to love me," but they never think about their own sex. They look for the perfect man or the perfect woman, when that *person*, quote unquote, could be sitting right next to them. But because of whatever stereotypes or biases they have, they don't look. They think that that perfect person is going to be in the opposite sex. That's not the case sometimes. (Lois Hayes)

Three men had adopted a "chosen" account as an articulated philosophy, quite at odds with their actual experience in becoming gay. They do not follow the logic used by the "mixed" account respondents; early feelings for men and lack of the same for women are not signs of an underlying, and unchosen, orientation. Thus, although in their pasts they never felt that being gay was a choice, and they could not now identify actual choices they had made, these respondents offer idiosyncratic accounts to claim that they had *really* chosen, and had actually made choices that they were unaware of.

Brian Polaski is a 31-year-old white man with a bachelor's degree who reads philosophy, writes poetry, and makes a living as a secretary. He was the third of five children in a comfortable and staunchly Catholic working-class home. He was considered a "sissy boy."

I had been persecuted by schoolmates in a perhaps typical way for a sissy boy, bad at sports. And you know, called "faggot" and all that.

But Brian did not think of himself as gay, and his earliest sexual feelings and experiences were heterosexual.

> I had heterosexual fantasies though most of my teens, and in fact had a girlfriend in high school for four years, with whom I had some type of a sexual relationship.

He experienced what he calls an "internal metamorphosis" over the course of his first year in college. He felt a new attraction to men and began to find sex with his girlfriend more and more unpleasant.

> BP: I came out in New York, and I think that somehow the geo-
>   graphic stride of fording the Hudson was a—, I crossed a bound-
>   ary line which allowed me to reconstruct my personality. I was in
>   an all-male dorm. And there were men who were out, on my
>   floor. And I was very drawn to them. I started to bottom out on
>   my girlfriend. Sexual contact with her became more and more
>   repugnant. And started to unleash my unconscious with a lot of
>   grotesque imagery. I would kind of be in bed with her, and my
>   head would be full of marshland, populated by frogs and reptiles.
>   While I was in bed with her. And then these fantasies about boys
>   became more and more solid in my mind, or fully developed.
> VW: The heterosexual fantasies, what became of them?
> BP: They expired, between the ages of eighteen and twenty.

At the time, he experienced this metamorphosis as beyond his control.

> It wasn't an issue in the sense that I deliberated about it. It was a trauma, in the sense that I had trouble with it, but it wasn't like a con-scious act. It was like some type of regeneration, or transformation that I went through, in a fairly chaotic way.

But today Brian states that he has chosen to be gay. His interest in existentialism shines through his explanation of his belief that "we make ourselves gay."

> I tend to think that choice is all important, freedom of choice. I feel less and less sympathetic with psychological theories of causality, even ordinary Freudian ones, that, you know, we suffer from our pasts, and are compelled by them. I sort of believe in this possibility of infinite instantaneous liberation from any kind of past, in a moment of absolute choice. And I think that we reiterate these choices on a day-by-day basis. So that we make ourselves gay every time we do

something gay. And should, you know, the mood come over us, I think that you or I could walk out of here and go out to a straight singles bar and you know, be neck and neck by tomorrow morning with people who've been at it for years. So I'm not a determinist. (Brian Polaski)

These three men, each following an idiosyncratic philosophy, believe that homosexuality is a choice even though, unlike Diane above or the feminists quoted below, they cannot identify the process whereby they actually made the choice.

Before I realized that homosexuality is a choice I didn't think about it much. But I would've fallen back on [the belief that it is not a choice] as a crutch if someone had attacked me. I would've said "this is the way I am, this is the way I was born." Now I see it as a choice. I don't think it's important that people go back and try to find the day or the hour or the period of time that they made the choice. It's not that conscious because of the world we live in. It can't be that conscious, we won't let it be. (Henry Yount)

A conscious choice for me is, "What gives me the greatest pleasure?" I feel better, more aroused, I feel more vigorous, more energetic, just more fulfilled, with a man than I do with a woman. If I had never met anyone who was homosexual, or who wanted to have a sexual relationship, I might be married with a house full of kids at the moment. If I never knew that it was there. At first, enjoyment with the women was much more than enjoyment with the guys. But it shifted, simply because the pleasure became greater someplace else. So I don't think you're born gay or straight. I think you are born with the potential for enjoying whatever it is that kind of fits in, and gives you the most pleasure, is where you're going to go. That's a little like Skinner, I think in a way. (Edward Potter)

Although all three recognize that sexual feelings are not always voluntary, Henry, Edward, and Brian at bottom do not believe that sexual orientations exist as such. For each of the three, there is only preference, chosen and amenable to change. They applied that philosophy to others, claiming that other gay men and lesbians also choose homosexuality, but aren't aware of it.

So I began to think about choice, and why we're not permitted to see it as a choice, and why it's not talked about as a choice. If you ask most homosexuals, they'll say "No, I didn't have a choice; I was born this way." (Henry Yount)

Edward Porter, a white 48-year-old school teacher currently working on a graduate degree, takes the most extreme position. For him, behavior is the only thing that's real, and so his definition of "gay" is one-dimensional.

> EP: My friends says, "You're either straight or gay." And I say that's not true. I am not, twenty-four hours a day, a sexually oriented person. It's at those times when I am going to be sexual, it is homosexual. The only time I'm gay, is basically when I have a relationship with someone.
>
> VW: So you might even say that relationships are gay, not that people are gay.
>
> EP: Oh, I like that.

The remaining "chosen" account respondents are those women who made the choice to be lesbians in a feminist context. They do not claim that an underlying bisexuality informed the choice, although many make a point of mentioning that they had not been unable to relate sexually and emotionally to men prior to their coming out. They frame the decision as a politically informed choice between involvement with men and with women, and portray lesbianism as a general, not solely sexual, preference for women.

> I think of a lesbian as a person who identifies more with women, and the preferred people to be around are women, and I've always been that way. I didn't become sexually involved with women until two years ago, so I would say that other people looking in would say I became a lesbian two years ago. (Sara Pritchard)

Anna Blumberg is a 36-year-old, college-educated lesbian who works in a hospital lab. She is the oldest of four children born to a middle-class Jewish family on Long Island. She was "never a tomboy," and she was attracted to boys throughout her teenage years. She became seriously involved with a man her first year of college.

> I loved him, but I didn't have the same kind of passion for him as I had in earlier years for guys that I was just hung up over. But my relationships that have lasted have not been the passionate relationships. He and I were that kind of relationships where we could've lived together, and made a home together, or something, and loved each other, but without a lot of passion.

In 1971, at the end of the relationship's first year, Anna became active in the feminist movement on campus. That began the process through which she became a lesbian.

AB: I was getting involved in all these feminist ideas, and I remember that there was a level on which he and I couldn't communicate, and I didn't get the things from him that I wanted. And I remember there was one time in particular that I asked to him to do something sexual and he just couldn't do it. And I just said, you know, it took another week or so, before I said, "I really don't like this." We stopped being lovers at that point. And then I said to myself, I mean for me it was a real thought-out process, "Well, now that I know that I don't want to be with men, can I be attracted to women?" And then I realized, within about a month, that I could be attracted, I was attracted to my roommate. And then probably a month later I fell in love with a woman I knew. We stayed together for three-and-a-half years.

VW: So you started with splitting off from him, and then—

AB: [*finishes my sentence*]: —seeing other possibilities.

Anna is quite certain that she chose to be a lesbian.

> [Before I became a feminist], it wasn't something that I was very much aware of, the possibility. But I was choosing that I didn't want to be with men, and then later I chose that I did want to be with women. I was very excited, I was really happy.

Like Anna, all the respondents in this group made thoughtful, deliberate choices to become lesbians.

> I was really tired of playing games with men. I was hip to sexism so long ago, and because of that my idea of what sexism was and how much I, as an individual, have to take was real limited, and I think I'd overstepped the boundaries. And finally one day I said, "You know what, I just want a person, a human being." And finally the words came to me, "You want a person? You didn't say you wanted a man, did you? Not a man? What is it for God's sake?" You know, "Could it be a woman?" (Adrienne DuBois)

> I guess it was sort of a political decision. It was back around '74, and I was very involved with the women's liberation movement, and I realized that there wasn't a place for men in my life, and also that I needed something about women that I wasn't sure of, but knew that I needed. It wasn't as if I was always having terrible relationships with men. I did have some good experiences, you know. But I felt like there was much more to what I was experiencing with women. (Virginia Bradford)

> Before I started calling myself a lesbian, I was thinking—I don't know where I had read this, about political lesbianism, or women-identification, I guess. And because I had taken a lot of women's studies coursework, I was beginning to say, "Yeah, that's exactly what I'm thinking; that's exactly where I'm coming from right now. It's just that I won't be sexual with women, so I guess I'm a political lesbian, or whatever." This is before I came out. (Mary Behnke)

> I guess the women in my life were becoming more important to me in different ways, and that was a process that had been going on for the last several years. I was, I guess I was becoming more comfortable with the idea of being a lesbian. Or being with lesbians. I think I was just in a place where I was receptive to it. (Pearl Johnson)

All the women who chose to be lesbian in a feminist context are conscious of their difference from other lesbians.

> I didn't go through a tortured childhood, or a tortured high-school-hood, in the sense that I really wanted to do something but I was with men because I thought I had to. You know, I didn't really go through that kind of thing, so I don't understand it. I was at a workshop at a women's music festival last year, and I was shocked at how guilty and tense some women feel about being gay. (Sara Pritchard)

A few suggest that this makes them outsiders in some way; Adrienne DuBois, a 32-year-old black realtor from Queens, knows that some lesbians would not consider her the genuine article.

> I'm not going to spend a lot of time forgiving myself or forgiving anybody else because I started out straight, damn it. Okay? I say to people, "You're going to have to take me as I am. I am converted, if you wish, okay? I used to be straight, now I'm gay. I'm sorry if it would make you happy that I was born this way, but I wasn't."

While they may be sensitive to it, these women find the distinction between real and false lesbians an artificial one. So is even the distinction between lesbians and heterosexual women. They compare themselves to straight women, and refer to the forces that keep women in particular behaving heterosexually—forces that they overcame in some way.

> When I was a kid I was going through the idea that any woman can be a lesbian. I still think lots of women could be. Lots could. I think that there's some people it would just horrify so much. (Libby Markowitz)

I think a lot of women are straight because the choice of being a lesbian is too difficult, being made too difficult by society. So I think a lot of women overlook their inclinations that are telling them they want to be with women, but they're saying no, they can't be, because it's too difficult. (Virginia Bradford)

I have friends who are straight, you know. I realize it's problematical for them because they have not been able to get out of where I was at, at that particular trap. I think of heterosexuality as a kind of a trap. And they can't get out of that trap. I've been known to say, "I think you would be better off without men." And some women say to me, "I just can't bring myself to do that." And I tell them all, "I don't expect you to make any compromises on my account. It's *your* life." But culture and society says you sleep with men if you're a woman. (Adrienne DuBois)

The feminists who offer the "chosen" account speak in terms that suggest they do not experience their sexuality as an orientation. These women do not talk about discovering their true sexualities, or finding out that they were really lesbians. Similarly, "any woman can be a lesbian," or at least many women could be, and it's not a matter of finding out what their sexual orientation is; it's a matter of making a choice. Once Anna, Pearl, Adrienne and the others nurtured their political and emotional preferences for women into a sexual preference, they became lesbians. If orientations exist for them, they can be shaped by preferences. As such, being and doing interact and shape one another, and cannot be neatly partitioned. Libby Markowitz, a 28-year-old Jewish woman from Long Island who works as a forest ranger, describes the process of developing a lesbian orientation.

LM: I didn't *know* that I was a lesbian, but I wanted to be one. I used to say I was a political lesbian because I hadn't had a lover yet. I had my best friend, but I wasn't attracted to her and I was waiting for when I would be attracted to women.

VW: So what happened then to make you sure this was for you?

LM: I worked at it. I was like wanting the possibility. So I started working on the lesbian paper, and going to concerts and the coffeehouse, and I met my first lover. So that made all the difference to really have a lover and really fall in love with somebody.

Unlike the idiosyncratic men, these lesbians experienced their coming out as a choice at the time, and not only in a philosphically informed recasting of the past. But that doesn't mean they were always perfectly consistent. When confronted with the dangers of choice, some would temporarily depart from their "chosen" account, to avail themselves of the defenses summoned by eschewing choice.

RV: My old boyfriend said, "Well, Rosa, the truth of the matter is
that you didn't have a lesbian sexual experience until after you
had that really bad sexual experience with me." You know?
Another one of those assholes that thinks that he's the reason
why everyone does everything in their life. So I'm like, "Yeah,
well, I guess—. Hey! Wait a minute!" And then I started thinking, you know, "Well, there was Lorna, and there was Lettie,"
and I'm thinking back and I'm going, "Yeah, I had lesbian experiences when I was a kid!" And going, "Hey, maybe there's more
to this than I know about." It took him saying something rude
like that, for me to remember that, yup, I had lesbian sexual
experiences back then.

VW: When you first came out you didn't think about those things?

RV: No. I didn't remember; I totally didn't remember. (Rosa Velez)

When I had been involved with Katharine I was like deciding to be
involved with her, but it was like a choice with no heartfelt desire, or
whatever. And a lot of that came out of the fact that a lot of straight
friends I had had previously decided they were lesbians. People were
sort of reexamining their feminist politics in light of lots of lesbian
theory that they were reading, and lesbian literature. You know, it was
kind of where it was at, sort of. But when I became really attracted to
Carol, it seemed more like something I was discovering about myself.
(Pearl Johnson)

Rosa invokes determinism to counteract an accusation that she became a lesbian because of a man, and Pearl invokes it to distinguish herself from those
whose lesbianism was merely "where it's at."

Clearly there is less coherence to the "chosen" category than the other two.
Theirs are the alternative voices, whose variation from the dominant account
comes from a variety of sources. A few men are idiosyncratic; they hold to one
belief system or another that values choice, and so they claim it for their own
accounts. Some men and women refer to an underlying bisexual orientation
that allowed them to choose between men and women. And a good number of
women tell of choosing to become lesbians after feminism changed their lives
and their worldviews. However dissimilar, all have accounted for their homosexuality by stating that it is "chosen," and all are aware that this makes them a
minority within a minority.

Account Dominance

The evidence suggests that the "mixed" account is the dominant approach among
gay men and lesbians. This sample of respondents is not, of course, randomly

selected. As such, its statistical contours bear an unknown mathematical relationship to the statistical contours of the lesbian and gay population of the U.S. Nonetheless, the predominance of this type of account among these respondents does indicate something about the world beyond the sample. First, nothing about sampling procedures suggests that people who share this belief would be oversampled. Some of my recruitment efforts did ask specifically for people who had "chosen to be gay/lesbian," and some "mixed"-account respondents did answer those calls, along with the "chosen"-account respondents for whom I was searching. But these ads and flyers were distributed specifically because the general calls for lesbian and gay volunteers were being answered almost exclusively by people whose accounts were of the "mixed" type. The fact that individuals offering this account answered both general and specific calls for volunteers suggests that their beliefs represent the dominant thinking.

Second, their tendency to believe that all gay men and lesbians shared their beliefs and experiences suggests cultural dominance. The majority of those who offered a "mixed" account assume that other lesbians and gay men share their beliefs and experience. Half the women and nearly all the men expressed the belief that their experience is universal.

> [When asked if she chose to be a lesbian]: I feel that it's a conscious choice to accept what I am, that's my choice. The choice of being a lesbian—there's no choice in that, it's a fact.
> [When asked if other lesbians choose]: No, I don't think so, no. Everybody sort of feels we are. Just a fact. (Katie Lee)

> [Regarding herself:] I feel like I did make the choice to discover who I am, but I didn't at all make the choice to be gay.
> [Regarding others:] No, again, I think it's the kind of thing that we are, and then we realize that we are. (Sharon Halpern)

> It's the lifestyle I chose. I think most gay men have the same feeling. (Thomas Labadan)

> I think people who have chosen to do gay, or lesbian, might think that they chose to be, because they're not, they don't understand the difference between being and doing. (Al Davis)

> I think that for most people it's something that is an aspect of themselves, that they have not chosen.... I think the things we desire are, the desires come from within us. It's not something we choose to desire. The lifestyle may be a choice, but not the actual desire. (Robert Henderson)

Although the "determined" account differed from the "mixed" account, the male respondents who offered the former also saw their experience as representing the universal gay man/person:

> I don't think I ever decided; it just sort of happened. It's not a decision anybody makes—you're just born that way. (Dan Bartlett)

> I think people are born gay. From what I know from myself, and just from talking to other people. It seems like they knew at an early age. (Brent McKenna)

In contrast, the women who offer the Determined account recognize that theirs is not the experience of all lesbians. Some suggest that their experience was "easier" or less ambiguous than that of most lesbians.

> VW: Do you feel that you were born a lesbian?
> JD: Yes.
> VW: Do you think most lesbians are born lesbians?
> JD: I think it's fifty-fifty. My lover started having feelings about women when she was 16. And assumed like every other woman I know who eventually becomes gay, that "a good male will straighten me right out." (Justine DiAngelo)

An androcentric culture encourages men to understand themselves as generically human, to be sure. But the men who gave the "chosen" account did not, so account type and gender interact here. The "determined" account is much closer to the "mixed" account than is the "chosen" account. The basic agreement that a homosexual orientation is not chosen links the "determined" and "mixed" accounts, making them versions of the same dominant account. All the respondents who did not give some version of the dominant account saw themselves as exceptions.

Why do lesbians and gay men select a particular account? For these accounts are truly stories of choice, told not only about choice, but by choice. And they are chosen for reasons far more complex than simply representing one's experience. The few respondents' stories told in this chapter suggests that experiences vary widely, while account statements are remarkably similar. The next chapter will begin looking at why these respondents elect to use their "determined," "chosen," or "mixed" accounts.

Notes

1. In the course of the interview, which focused on the respondent's coming-out story, I asked, "To what extent do you feel being gay/lesbian is a conscious choice you have made?" Respondents were also asked for their opinions about choice in the lives of lesbians and gay men in general. The concept of choice often appeared elsewhere in the interviews as well. Table 2 summarizes the number of male and female respondents who used each account type. These numbers are presented to describe the sample; they do not constitute a finding *per se*.

Table 2: Typology of Accounts			
Account type	**Men**	**Women**	**Total**
Determined	5	4	9
Mixed	22	23	45
Chosen	6	12	18
	33	39	72

2. Variation in gay male identities has rarely been studied, but research on lesbian identities provides some models for understanding individual women's different paths to lesbianism. Ponse's (1978) groundbreaking research distinguished "primary," "elective," and "idiosyncratic" lesbian identities. Ettore (1980) categorized lesbians as "born" and "self-chosen." Most recently, Burch (1993) analyzed the relationship dynamics between "primary" and "bisexual" lesbians.

3. See Thomas Weinberg (1983) for a thorough treatment of these "indicators," or "indexical particulars," of homosexuality.

four

Choosing a Story: Determined, Chosen, and Mixed

Determined and Chosen Accounts

The lesbians and gay men who use the "determined" account and those who use the "chosen" account are distinguished by more than just their beliefs about the source of their sexual preferences; for the most part these different accounts reflect very different life experiences. Perhaps the central differentiating experience is continuity: "determined"-account respondents recall an unbroken sense that they were homosexual from an early age, while those who offer the "chosen" account do not claim this continuity of identity.[1] The "chosen" account group also has more heterosexual experience and fewer members who recall childhood gender nonconformity. A few respondents present exceptions to these patterns, but generally these two groups' accounts reflect their experiences in a logical way.

I invited respondents to begin telling me their stories by asking, "Could you tell me how you came to decide that you are gay/a lesbian?" a wording I had chosen to avoid limiting respondents to the essentialist language of knowledge and discovery. But it was a wording soundly rejected by most of the nine individuals who offered the "determined" account, in favor of language that referred more directly to an underlying orientation.

> I don't think I ever decided. It just sort of happened. It's not a decision anybody makes, you're just born that way. (Dan Bartlett)

Whether or not they resisted using the term "decide," "determined" account respondents answered my query with some version of the statement, "I always knew." With only one exception, all of them made it clear that their homosexuality was continuous; they became aware of it at or before puberty, and they never self-identified as anything but homosexual. Although they never changed identities, and never experienced a momentous discovery, there certainly were turning points where their awareness intensified and their identities crystallized. Many recall learning a word—"gay," "homosexual," "lesbian," "faggot"—and recognizing themselves in it.

> When I was about fourteen there was a bookmobile that used to come by in the summertime, so I started reading up on sexuality. And it wasn't long before I came across homosexuality and I thought, "Then that must be me." (Malcolm Wilson)

But it was their understanding that changed, not their feelings. These respondents describe a continuous knowledge of an underlying homosexual orientation.

> I had known since the time I was four years old that I was gay. I always had these sexual feelings toward men. And I figured that maybe it was a normal thing to do, to be that way. I've always felt that way. (Eric Lehman)

> I have been gay all my life. I had no real coming out because I can distinctly remember having gay imagery, gay thoughts, that I can now see were gay, as early as five. There was never any doubt in my mind as to what I was interested in. (William Sloan)

Most believe they were born gay.

> I think I've been gay from birth. And I've never had a heterosexual experience. And I've never had the desire to have one, so I guess you could say I'm gay to the full extent. (Malcolm Wilson)

Only one of the "determined"-account respondents did not experience continuity in his homosexuality. His story is somewhat unusual, for although he did not always know he was gay, he does not recall an onset of awareness. He reconciles these two somewhat contradictory claims by using the concept of "drift." Dan Bartlett, a 51-year-old architect from a white, Protestant, and upper-class Manhattan family, describes a process that was slow but inevitable.

> VW: So do you remember when you first said to yourself, "I'm gay"?

DB: I don't think I ever did. You don't say that. I think it was proba-
     bly when I was twenty years old, when I had my first big affair.

VW: That was a turning point?

DB: Yeah, but it was never anything momentous. Just sort of hap-
     pened. It's not something I ever thought about. It just seemed
     very natural to just sort of slide into it. I was also having sex
     with women, and up until I was about twenty, I didn't think of
     myself as anything but having a good time. I never thought of
     myself as either one or the other.

Dan's ability to "slide," to be sexually active for a period of years without self-
labeling, is unusual, as he is well aware.

> The way I came out and so on was just so much more relaxed than a
> lot of people go through.

Although Dan's story departs from the others', he is with them in his firm belief
that he was born gay. When Dan says he did not choose to be gay, he means he
never exercised any choices; he drifted into a gay life without experiencing the
lifelong sense of sexual difference to which the other "determined"-account
respondents refer. Dan demonstrates the absence of choice in one sense—the
actual exercise of choice—while the other "determined" respondents define
choice differently—as the existence of other viable options (see Card 1995).

In contrast, nearly all the eighteen respondents who offered the "chosen"
account experienced a discontinuity between their gay and pre-gay selves. They
initially identified as heterosexual, then changed to a gay or lesbian identity in
their teens or twenties.[2] Most now embrace their discontinuous pasts, and avoid
defining their previous identities as false.

VW: So while you were going through this [coming-out] process, did
     you find yourself looking back at your past in a different way?

PJ: You mean was I in love with my gym teacher? (We *laugh*.) Not
     a lot. I mean it explained some things in terms of dealing with
     boys I guess, when I was a teenager and stuff. But a lot of that
     was just fucked-up stuff that happens when you're a teenager,
     and you have to deal with boys. I think that heterosexual—girls
     that feel pretty heterosexual, or that eventually end up claiming
     that identity, or whatever, probably had the same experiences,
     you know? (Pearl Johnson)

> When I first came out to my high-school friends, one of them said to
> me, "Oh yeah, you always said that you loved us." So she thought that

maybe I'd always been gay. But you know, you love your girlfriends. (Anna Blumberg)

VW: Do you remember looking back on earlier years of your life and seeing them differently?

VB: Not entirely, but to some extent. It wasn't as if I was always having terrible relationships with men. I did have good experiences, you know, really nice ones. But I felt like there was much more to what I was experiencing with women.

VW: So you didn't feel like your life up to then had been all wrong or something like that?

VB: No. (Virginia Bradford)

VW: Do you remember, when you came out, looking back on your life differently?

BP: Not much. With the exception of the playground persecution I referred to [earlier in interview]. In *St. Genet*, Sartre makes the claim that the young Jean being called a thief, which Genet records, at a very puerile level, while he was a very little boy, was a type of stigma that he thereafter came to fulfill. And I wondered to what degree being named created an existence for me. (Brian Polaski)

These claims use the other side of the logic demonstrated in Chapter Three, where respondents present early evidence of homosexuality to prove that they could not have chosen to be gay. Having selected the "chosen" account, these respondents do not present evidence of early homosexuality; they pass up the opportunity to attribute such meaning to their pasts. But there are two exceptional cases that are counterintuitive, two respondents who simultaneously claim to have chosen their homosexuality and to have always been aware of it.

Henry Yount, the one man of the "chosen" group who claims a continuous knowledge of his homosexuality, is a 45-year-old white man, originally from rural Pennsylvania, who works as a freelance copyeditor. He belongs to a small group in New York City that studies and practices the ideas of a gay psychiatrist who claimed that homosexuality is a choice (Rosenfels 1971). (The group's primary activity is the operation of therapy circles and rap groups designed to teach his philosophies to participants. I interviewed another respondent who had participated in a few of these sessions and was not compelled by them.) Henry explains his position with certainty:

It was as a result of running into this group that I began to take my homosexuality much more seriously. I began to think a lot about choice, and why we're not permitted to see it as a choice, and why it's not talked about as a choice. If you ask most homosexuals, they'll say, "No, I didn't have a choice. I was born this way."

But in spite of taking this position, Henry tells a story of "always knowing."

> I've been sexually attracted to my peers beginning around age ten. There were actual incidents. I of course saw that as some kind of deviation that would pass, or something like that. I remember specifically when I was thirteen, fourteen, all the boys who were involved in this activity kind of moving away from it, and me wondering why that wasn't happening to me.

The two strands of his narrative exist alongside one another. He explains the apparent contradiction by maintaining that, in a homophobic and heterosexist context, we make choices without being aware of them. While, as we will see below, many "mixed" account respondents claim that they were "always gay but unaware of it," Henry reverses the terms, claiming that he chose to be gay but was unaware of doing so, having made an "unconscious choice." So although he did not actually experience his homosexuality as a choice he is now fully convinced that it was.

> I don't think it's important that people go back and try to find the day or the hour or the period of time that they made the choice. It's not that conscious because of the world we live in. It can't be that conscious; we won't let it be.

Tina Fiore, the one "chosen" lesbian who claims continuous awareness, is a 40-year-old white woman from a working-class background who currently works as a retail clerk. After twenty years identifying and living as a lesbian, she is considering becoming involved with a man. She adamantly resists claiming that her lesbian history was inauthentic or mistaken, just as the other "chosen" respondents resist making that claim about their heterosexual experience.

> VW: So what do you currently think of as your sexual identity? Do you still think of yourself as a lesbian, or—?
>
> TF: I was thinking about that last night. I think that if I were to say, "No, I'm not a lesbian," then that would be sort of like saying that none of it was real. That my relationships were not real to me, and that's not true. I think that it doesn't matter to me anymore? I think that I'm just more, um, interested in who I feel is more compatible.

> VW: What would you have said, say five years ago?
>
> TF: Five years ago I would've said, "I'm a lesbian."

As with the other "chosen" lesbians, Tina's claim of choice allows her to embrace and explain the changes and discontinuities in her life course. But unlike the others, she tells a story about "always knowing" alongside a story about being bisexual, and exercising various choices.

> VW: When did you first start thinking of yourself as a lesbian?
> TF: Oh, god. Actually, the truth is, when I was in third grade, I had a dream about one of my teachers. I loved this woman so much (*chuckles*). I can always remember feeling that I wanted to be with a woman. Always felt that. Even when I dated guys, I always knew in the back of my mind that it was a woman I wanted to be with. When the opportunity finally came, I took it. And I always knew it would come, and I always knew I would take it.
> VW: So could you have chosen not to take it?
> TF: I could have, but I also felt that if I didn't like it, that I could always walk away from it. I didn't feel that it was anything I had to commit myself to. 'Cause I, you know, I just didn't feel that way. This is interesting, because I knew that if it was something that I didn't want to commit myself to, I could just walk away from it. And here I am, (*laughs*), saying "Well gee, all those things didn't go the way I really wanted them to." But anyway, I don't regret it.

That her story is currently under revision shows through this narrative. The claim that she always knew she was attracted to women is fleshed out with detailed childhood memories—a crush on a teacher, what she felt when she was dating boys. Her claim that she always felt she could go either way is worded more vaguely and lacks supportive detail. Tina seems to be revising her opinions as well, as illustrated in the following quotation. She initially asserts that people are born with their sexual preferences, and then backs away from that statement, step-by-step, until she arrives at an opinion that is in accord with her current situation.

> VW: Do you think that people are born with their sexual preference?
> TF: I do. I think that if they're not born with it—maybe we're not born with much of anything, except your flesh—but it happens months after birth. I really believe that. I really believe that we see and hear and smell and taste all these things, and as an infant you can decide what you like and don't like. Even though at that time they're just sensations, but they really form the basis of choices as adolescents.

VW: So do you think that's something that's set then, once that happens in first year or so?

TF: Set? I think if you're unlucky they become set. I don't think that it's that good to—, I wouldn't want to think that things are set. I think that you know intuitively the atmosphere of the rest of the life you would like to have. But I don't think it's healthy to say, "This is the way it's going to be, no matter what." 'Cause then you don't question what you're about.

Tina's unusual pattern—claiming both continuity and a "chosen" account—is part of her unusual life history, and part of a story that seems to be currently under revision. If she ever feels the need to tell a more internally consistent story, she may add more detail to her claims that she always knew she could choose either women or men. That is, she may claim that she always knew she was bisexual. But as a relatively isolated person, she experiences less pressure than many to tell a consistent story. Generally, the women who offer the "chosen" account tell a fairly consistent story, one that does not feature some underlying sexual orientation of which they "always knew."

Nearly all of the "determined" account respondents report that others recognized them as homosexual, or as "different," early on, a report which none of the "chosen" respondents makes.

> I've sat down and talked to my brothers, and my brothers have said that they knew something was wrong when I was a child. Something was different about me. When given a choice of dolls or trucks I went to the trucks. It's just the way I've always been, I never thought about being any other way. I think I was born gay, I say it from the get-go. I think it was meant for me to be this way. (Sandie Martin)

> I was seven years old, and I came home crying because the other boys called me a sissy. And my mother said—and to this day, I'm so grateful to my mother for saying this—she said, "Well, that's just the way you are, so there's no need to cry about it. You just have to be the way you are and every time they say that, you say, 'Yes, I am, and that's the way I am; there's nothing I can do about it, and I don't care.'" And I said, "Well, I guess that's it." And every time they said that I said, "Yes, I am," and they went, "Oh." And they never called me that again because they said, "We're not getting the reaction anymore." At that time, I needed what she said. I credit that with a lot of my sort of self-fulfillment as a gay man to this day. (Malcolm Wilson)

As Sandie's and Malcolm's quotations suggest, when "determined"-account respondents say they or others "always knew," they often are referring to an early awareness that they were less feminine than other girls, or less masculine than other boys. Here respondents invoke the well-established common sense belief that sissy boys, and to a less predictable extent tomboy girls, will mature into homosexual adults. Justine's anecdote has a mythical quality, like a Mojave "bow or burden-strap" story (in which a male infant's attraction to women's rather than men's tools is a sign of his gender-crossing destiny).

> I felt for the longest time that there was something wrong with me because I feel I have this little boy running around inside me, not this little girl. I mean I remember growing up and my father calling me "Butch," as a nickname. I think it all started when I was very little and I first learned how to walk. The first thing I did is I wandered into the tool cellar and started playing with the tools. I was just naturally drawn to things like that. (Justine DiAngelo)

Of the "determined" group, only Dan and Terry have no such memories of childhood gender nonconformity.

> I was never a tomboy. I wasn't good enough (*laughs*). I mean I tried, but I couldn't do anything. I was like, "Oh, yeah, I'll try." Then I get hit in the head. (Terry Breiner)

The "chosen" account group was least likely to recall childhood gender non-conformity. Of the men, only Brian identifies as a childhood sissy.

> I had been persecuted by schoolmates in a perhaps typical way for a sissy boy, bad at sports. And you know, called "faggot" and all that. (Brian Polaski)

Even though he owns to having been a sissy boy, he does not treat it as an indicator of underlying homosexuality, as he explains in the passage in which he invokes Sartre's *St. Genet.* A few of the "chosen" lesbians indicate that they were tomboys, and like Brian (but *sans Sartre*) they do not see their history of gender nonconformity as indicative of early homosexuality. If anything, they see it as an indication of an inchoate childhood feminism.

> I know I definitely never fell into what the media represented as young girls. Though I came from a middle-class family, I always felt that I was different. Which in retrospect everybody thinks that they're different. And I always preferred to play with boys and I couldn't stand to be around girls. Because I wore pants and most lit-tle girls wore dresses, and they didn't like to do the things that I liked

to do, more active types of things. And girls made me feel sort of inadequate, because they were a certain way and I felt I should be that way. I didn't want to be that way, as much as I felt I should be that way. (Sara Pritchard)

In Chapters Two and Three, some respondents supported their assertions that they did not choose their homosexuality. They point out that behaving heterosexually was not an option for them. As this reasoning would lead one to expect, the "determined" group has less heterosexual experience than the others; just half of these respondents report any at all. Some recall that they enjoyed heterosexual sex,[3] but less than with a partner of their own gender.

I actually liked girls. I was having a good time, and enjoying sex with women as well. Not as much as men, but I guess there was a period, actually, at about eighteen, nineteen, when there were more girls than boys. (Dan Bartlett)

I've had sexual relationships with men, but the feeling wasn't there, the heart, caring wasn't there. Sex was good but that was about it. (Sandie Martin)

Others report that they never liked it.

I had a girlfriend for a short time in high school, because she really desperately wanted it. We had sex but that wasn't very successful. (Brent McKenna)

I dated a man when I was fourteen, fifteen years old. Because I started to feel, "Well, maybe I am the only one. And maybe there is something wrong with me. And maybe if I date everybody in my family will get off my back about when am I gonna start dating." So I dated a man. From the first time he kissed me to the last time he kissed me, it didn't feel right. I couldn't kiss him. I tried to get myself to be sexual with him, and it was a fight. So I stopped. (Justine DiAngelo)

As Sandie's quotation suggests, what was missing from heterosexual sex was often as much emotional as physical. Only one respondent in the "determined" group has ever been involved in a meaningful heterosexual relationship; Dan dated a woman for two years in college. Some of the others occasionally dated for show, but never connected emotionally. Respondents who use the "determined" account are considerably less likely to have heterosexual experience than those who gave the "mixed" or "chosen" accounts. And unlike many respondents in the other two groups, none of those who used the "determined" account ever thought of themselves as bisexual, even for a short time.

VW: So did you ever go through a period of thinking of yourself as
        bisexual?
EL: Never. Absolutely not, ever, ever. (Eric Lehman)

Those who offer the "chosen" account have more heterosexual experience
than those who offer the "determined" account. All of the "chosen" men, and all
but two of the "chosen" women, have sexual experience with at least one person
of the other gender. Nearly all say that their heterosexual experiences were enjoy-
able, but usually less so than their homosexual ones.

> I was involved on and off with the same woman for eighteen years.
> And she was better in bed than eighty-five percent of the guys I've
> ever been with. But with men, a small percent of them, the emotion
> has been so great that I would not care to settle for anything else.
> (Edward Porter)

> I had been with men sexually, and I had been with women sexually.
> Speaking of mere sexuality, I enjoyed both. It was emotionally that I
> nowhere felt the same at all with men as I did with women. (Lois
> Hayes)

> It was how I felt about, ultimately, about sexism that did it. I didn't
> think it was a matter of taste, because I wasn't backward as a hetero-
> sexual. I was crossing the line between heterosexual and homosex-
> ual, and I asked myself, "Is it a matter of taste?" And the answer was
> no, so I said, "It must be something else." (Adrienne DuBois)

"Chosen" account respondents were also more likely than others to have been
emotionally involved in a heterosexual relationship. Three women and two men
had been married, or had lived with a heterosexual partner for a year or more.
Sara Pritchard, a 29-year-old white woman from Seattle who is working on a
graduate counseling degree, says of the man she lived with for five years:

> We met in school and then moved to New York together.... When
> we split, it was not for lack of love. I just had to get out on my own.

As we saw in Chapter Three, three men and four women of the "chosen"-account
group see themselves as "basically bisexual," and ground their "chosen" account
on that claim. The rest ground their "chosen" account on something other than
bisexuality, but nonetheless are more likely than "determined" or "mixed"
respondents to believe that they have some bisexual potential. Many felt that they
could be bisexual if they really wanted to.

I think I could live a straight life. Or maybe bisexual. But it's hard for me to think about now because I absolutely don't want to. I've come so far from that. (Mary Behnke)

I called myself bisexual when I was married, but I think bisexuality is the state of not having made a choice. (Henry Yount)

Age usually approximates cohort, but in gay and lesbian worlds another type of cohort exists, comprising those who came out at the same time. Morton Phelps, who came out at the age of fifty after eighteen years of marriage, identifies with men half his age who came out when he did.

My wife and I split in June, and in July I called the Episcopal church and said, "I hear you have meetings for gay people." So I walked in, and it was me. It was where I belonged; it was who I was. And it was wonderful. A couple of them are still my friends. We consider ourselves the class of eighty-two, that's when we came out.

Although Morton uses the "mixed" rather than "determined" account, his quotation illustrates the importance of coming-out cohort, as distinct from age.

For men especially, the year 1969 marks the divide between two major cohorts, the pre- and post-Stonewall generations.[4] Although their ages range from 30 to 63, all but one of the men of the "determined"-account group are from the pre-Stonewall cohort. They came out young; the median age at which "determined"-account respondents first took on a gay identity is 14, compared to 20 for the "chosen" group. All but one of the "chosen" group first took on a gay identity after 1969.

Very few of the women I interviewed came out before 1969, but Stonewall had less immediate effect on lesbians' than gay men's lives. The year 1980, which saw the first stirrings of the lesbian sexual revolution and the beginnings of lesbian-feminism's cultural decline, is probably more historically important. But cohort differences were slight between the "determined" and "chosen" lesbians. Although one might expect that the feminists would have all come out in the 1970s, during the heyday of lesbian-feminism, in fact half of them became lesbians after 1984. Most of the "determined" group came out over the course of the 1970s, but so did many of the "chosen" group. The two groups are, however, distinguished by the ages at which they came out. Where "determined"-account respondents typically "grew up gay" (the median age at which they came out is 12), "chosen"-account respondents tended to come out as young adults (median age: 20).

Because "determined"-account respondents usually adopted a gay identity when they were children, they came out in relatively isolated contexts—they knew no lesbians or gay men, and sought out information that might explain their feelings. The feminists who offer a "chosen" account, by contrast, became lesbians in a feminist atmosphere that supported their decisions. They were meeting, usually for the first time, other women who were lesbians, and other women who were questioning and changing their sexuality. The experience was not a matter of discovering that there were "others like themselves," as Malcolm Wilson did when he found the term "homosexuality" in a book. Rather, they did not feel they were attracted to women until they discovered that other women were. They discovered not only that lesbianism exists, but that it could offer them an entirely new way to understand their lives and their sexualities. As such, they lend much importance to the context of their coming-out experiences. Some begin their stories by reporting the context.

> VW: Could you tell me how you came to decide that you are a les-
> bian?
>
> AB: That was when I was twenty. I was going through pictures last
> night to remind myself (laughs). I first got involved in the
> women's movement.... (Anna Blumberg)

Most of the "chosen" lesbians who came out in a feminist context remain actively involved in lesbian community life, frequently taking part in lesbian gatherings in public space, including social, cultural, and political events, meetings, and the like.

Unlike these women, the "chosen" account men, and the "chosen" account women who claim an underlying bisexual orientation, came out in relatively isolated contexts. Only Diane Rivera, whose mother had many lesbian and gay friends, came out in a setting that acknowledged the viability of a homosexual way of being. Today, most of them remain fairly isolated, with few or no lesbian and gay friends, and little contact with any gay community life.[5]

> When I first came out, I didn't feel especially that I'd come home. I felt
> as alien in the gay environment as I did in most environments at the
> time. It's never really changed that much; I still feel alienated. (Rick
> Gross)

Although they have had many sexual partners, half of the "chosen" gay men have never been involved in a serious romantic relationship with another man, unlike the overwhelming majority of the men in the "determined" and "mixed" account groups. The bisexual "chosen" lesbians, following pattern more typical of women, have had lovers or are currently in a relationship, but are not a part of a public lesbian or gay community life. Lois Hayes describes the life she and her partner lead as "very private."

Marsha and I are very private people; we spend a lot of time to ourselves. We don't have many friends, we don't go out much. We're very
much into each other.

Coming out in an isolated context does not necessarily mean one will remain
there. Although all of the "determined"-account men came out on their own,
today all are very involved in gay community life; as a group they are among the
most socially and politically active people I interviewed. Most of the "determined"-account lesbians, on the other hand, have remained relatively isolated,
living private coupled lives such as Lois describes above. Table 3 summarizes the
various ways that "chosen" and "determined" respondents are and have been isolated from and integrated into gay and lesbian community life.

**Table 3: Coming Out Context by Current Integration
into Lesbian/Gay Community Life**

	Currently isolated	Currently integrated
Came out in isolated context	"Chosen" men "Determined" women bisexual "Chosen" women	"Determined" men
Came out in integrated context		feminist "Chosen" women

In some ways "chosen" and "determined" respondents' experiences are radically different: "determined" respondents "grew up gay," identifying in some way
as homosexual continuously from an early age, while "chosen" respondents did
not. "Chosen" respondents were considerably more likely than those who offer
the "determined" account to have experienced heterosexual relationships and
sexual encounters, and less likely to report that their childhood behavior crossed
gender boundaries. "determined" account respondents do not consider themselves bisexual and never did, while "chosen" account respondents—even those
who do not see themselves as "basically bisexual"—once identified as bisexual, or
believe they could develop a bisexual orientation if they wanted to. "Determined"
and "chosen" account respondents' relationships to lesbian and gay community
life, however, compare in more complicated ways that differ by gender (a topic
that will be addressed again below).

"Determined" and "chosen" accounts seem to reflect very different experiences, sometimes diverging early in respondents' lives. Many would conclude that
they represent different underlying orientations, following an argument that
would go something like this: Respondents who offer the "determined" account
do so because they actually were born gay or became so very early on. They are
exclusively and unalterably homosexual. Those who offer the "chosen" account,

on the other hand, are probably bisexually oriented, whether they know it or not, and the various stories they tell are just different ways of representing that. These two groups are truly different types of people, whose biologies or histories have left them with different internal configurations of sexual desire. My research is not designed to test such a hypothesis—if it could be tested at all—but I am generally disinclined to privilege such a "professional diagnosis" of an individual's sexuality over her own sense of it. What I will show is that the rest of the individuals I interviewed—the largest group, those using the dominant account—exhibit a much more complex relationship between experience and account, "underlying reality" and its "representation," and are more resistent to a facile judgment that they are distinguished by some shared underlying orientation.

The Mixed Account

Like those who use the "determined" account, many of the "mixed" account respondents resisted my use of the term "decide."

> VW: Could you tell me how you came to decide that you're gay?
> JM: I don't think I decided (*laughs*). I had kind of known for a long
>   time. (Jack Miklowicz)

> VW: Could you tell me when you came to decide that you're a lesbian?
> RD: I think I've always been a lesbian, but do you mean how I came to
>   decide that I would pursue it, or call myself a lesbian? (Rhia Dill)

Many of these respondents, like nearly all the "determined" group, had experienced continuous awareness of homosexual feelings. As Al and Gary put it, they "always knew."

> I always knew it was boys and men that got my interest. The first specific one of those that I remember was going to swimming class when I was seven or eight, and having college guys hold us in the water. I remember that I really keyed on the fact that these were men. I really liked that. But that was not like an awakening; I already knew that it was part of the pattern. So it was clearly from a real early stage. (Al Davis)

> It's a hard question. I guess I always knew. (Gary Perez)

Sometimes significant others recognized the young respondent as homosexual, or "different," an experience shared by most of the "determined" respondents as well.

> When I was thirteen, I sat my parents down. I said, "Look, I am very different from the other girls. You know I am, Dad. Just look at me.

You know!" I just knew all along. Then when I was fourteen I had this teacher who came on to me. I believe she saw gay in me. (Mara Pettinelli)

But not all "mixed"-account respondents experienced such continuity; some can recall a period before they were gay or lesbian—or, as they put it, before they *knew* they were. A few of these respondents who experienced discontinuity recall that their homoerotic feelings appeared after some years of feeling relatively asexual.

I never was sexual. And it wasn't until the senior year that I thought, "Hm, I wonder what I am?" I think I just started falling in love with men. Plus on top of it started the sexual feelings. So it was very clear. (Luke Hauser)

I knew when I was very young that I did not want to get married and did not want to have children, but I thought that I was going to be a nun. So I thought that I didn't want to get married and didn't want to have children because I was going to be a nun. It was very simple. Then, when I was nineteen I became friends with a woman who was a lesbian, but I didn't even know what it *was*. I had no idea that this existed, and I was fascinated to understand this.... [Later] I sat in the seminary library and said, "I think I'm gay." (Katie Lee)

Most experienced discontinuity by changing from a heterosexual to a gay identity. Their earliest sexual feelings were heteroerotic; these were supplemented or replaced by desires for members of their own gender.

Well, I didn't think about men in a sexual way, or feel attracted to them until I was almost 20 years old. At first I had a girlfriend. (Ralph Myers)

I went out with lots of different boys, I had no qualms about making out with every boy around. I was very promiscuous in that way. It never occurred to me that I could be doing that with girls. (Sharon Halpern)

Whether they were previously heterosexual or previously asexual, many "mixed"-4account respondents experienced a discontinuity in their sexualities. For the majority of such respondents, this separated their lives before and after becoming gay or recognizing their homosexuality. But for two women, the discontinuity was more complicated: Both grew up with some awareness of sexual interest in women but later became involved in serious relationships with men, and came to believe that they were no longer homosexual. This changed their sexual self-concepts. Years later, sexual desire toward women returned. So far they have come out, returned to straight life, and then come out again. Their accounts explain this rupture in what they otherwise see as a consistent lifelong sexual preference. Neither dismisses her heterosexual relationship entirely, but each portrays it as an aberration, and her return to lesbianism as inevitable.

> When I was eighteen, I put the name "gay" on it. But it was still like, "Uh, no, no, you can't be gay. No, no, no, you can't be like that." So I never did anything. I would sit and drool but that was it. And I ended up with the guy I married. I was with him for eight years.... I belonged to the bowling league, and there were a lot of lesbians on the bowling league. And then all of a sudden the feelings were coming back again. (Celia Daugherty, "mixed")

> CS: I went through a very weird time of falling for the wrong women. I got very, very fed up with everything, and that's how I met John. I was twenty-eight when we started living together.
> VW: So as the relationship went on, did you still think of yourself as a lesbian?
> CS: No. I also didn't think of myself as—I think I thought of myself as nothing, sexwise. I was living with a man who was like my father. He was like the father I always wanted....
> VW: Did you ever think of yourself as bisexual?
> CS: Yes. When I first met John. Because I liked him, I liked him a lot. After that period of where I couldn't find anybody and I was falling for all the wrong people, that's when I thought, "Maybe it's not the wrong people, maybe I'm with the wrong sex. Maybe I really should be with a man. Maybe I should give it a try." That's what I think John was all about, was giving it a try. In giving it a try, we developed a very strong relationship. (Cathy Saunders)

The other respondents experienced a simpler form of discontinuity, between their pre-gay and gay selves.

Table 4 below summarizes the three account-groups' experiences of continuity and discontinuity. As we have already seen, "determined"-account respondents generally "always knew," while "chosen"-account respondents have a discontinuous history of sexual self-understanding. The "mixed"-account group is divided, with a decided gender difference: Most of the women's homosexuality has been discontinuous, while most of the men experienced continuity.

Table 4: Account Type by Continuous Awareness of Homosexuality

GAY MEN[6]	Continuity	Discontinuity	Total
No Choice	4	1	5
Partial Choice	15	7	22
Total Choice	1	5	6
	20	13	33
LESBIANS[7]			
No Choice	4	0	4
Partial Choice	6	17	23
Total Choice	1	11	12
	11	28	39

Continuity/discontinuity is a dichotomous variable not only as I operationalize it, but as respondents use it as well. Many of those who report continuity asserted early in the interview that they "always knew," frequently using those very words. Others were just as quick to explain that they "didn't find out until later."[8]

Respondents of the "mixed" group who experienced discontinuity between their former and current sexualities treated that as a problem to be explained.

> The logical progression would seem to be that by the age of ten or eleven or twelve, I would have realized that I was gay. It's possible that it was entering my mind, but that for some reason I was blocking it out or saying no, but I don't remember that. (Robert Henderson, "mixed")

> I think for a long time I sort of felt something bad about myself because it took me so long to be a lesbian. I felt like, "What didn't I see? Why wasn't I more aware earlier?" I know initially I felt some embarrassment, because here I was twenty-eight or whatever. (Karen McNally, "mixed")

They were as likely as those who were continuously homosexual to believe that they were born gay.

> It's the way God made me. This is what he decided my course would be like. I think a lot of it's biological. I've sat down and thought about why are people like this, and I think a lot of it does have to do with biology. (Terence Metcalf)

> I'm more likely to believe we're born gay than to believe that we're not. I can't say it's not something we learn in the first year or two of

life, but I think it's probably something we're born with. (Robert Henderson)

Only a couple suggest that their discontinuous experience is evidence that they were not born gay. Cindy, who did not come to think of herself as a lesbian until her late twenties, here identifies a friend who came out much earlier as potentially born gay.

> I think in most people it's formed, but some people really do seem to be born a certain way. I have a friend, I think she was probably born gay. She came out very young. She's twenty-eight now, and I think she was fifteen when she knew it. (Cindy Schwartz)

All of the "mixed" respondents who experienced discontinuity explained it the same way, by invoking an underlying, continuous, and previously unknown homosexual orientation: They were always homosexual but didn't always know it. None believe they became homosexual at the same time that they discovered it. They gather evidence for this belief via retrospective interpretation (Schur 1979), a re-reading of their pre-homosexual pasts in terms of their present sexual identities.[9]

> VW: Could you tell me how you came to decide that you're a lesbian?
> KH: It was a fairly gradual process. Retrospectively, there were probably earlier indications of it, but the time I was really conscious was probably in my freshman year of college. It was just something that I had been missing that I just thought, "Oh, why didn't I think of that before?" (Kate Hargrave)

> I think—I mean in retrospect—I feel that I always was a lesbian. But I've only been out four or five years. It was this gradual process. I went to Catholic school for thirteen years, let me say that (laughs). (Karen McNally)

Many of these "mixed"-group respondents actively performed this recasting of the past as part of their coming out.

> When I came out I looked back on the types of games I liked to play as a child, or the kind of toys I wanted to have, or what my goals were. And I think I probably saw them differently. (Cindy Schwartz)

> AN: So some time around twenty I started realize that I was gay.

VW: Do you remember at that time looking back on events that had happened previously?

AN: Yes, oh yes, looking back to Billy in seventh grade, and David in fourth grade. Oh, yes. (Albert Ness)

DR: The year after I graduated from high school, this woman I was going with said, "Do you think you might be gay?" And without even thinking about it, I said, "Yeah." It was that simple, and then I just like took the ball and ran.

VW: Had you been thinking about it before she asked that?

DR: No.

VW: Did you surprise yourself answering that way?

DR: No. It was like immediately I went through my whole life, and took a whole inventory of like where that fit, where it fit into my life. (Dwight Russell, "mixed")

Their accounts must square a relatively late onset of "awareness" with a claim to a sexual orientation that was determined early on. As such, these respondents explain the discontinuity so as to explain it away, allowing them to claim that they were, in fact, always gay. Some use the language of denial and repression to explain away their pre-homosexual pasts:

I think I discovered something that I'd been hiding from myself. And I feel like I was discovering something that I knew since I was twelve years old. But I just never wanted to face up to it. (Sharon Halpern, "mixed")

SD: I've finally given up all the denial that I've gone through, and accepted it for myself. I think it got to the point where I was just getting as far as I could with denial and saying, "I don't want to be gay."

VW: You were actually saying that to yourself?

SD: Probably subconsciously. I don't think I was really doing it consciously. (Sol Davidoff, "mixed")

LH: In high school I was always looking at girls and thinking, "Oh, boy, I could fall in love with her." Not knowing anything about sex, or what that part of it was. But at one point, things started moving around, and I continued to have a couple of girlfriends, and realizing that that wasn't where I was.

VW: Why then?

LH: I was out of the house, out of my father's domination, I was allowed to be myself. By allowing myself to be myself, that part came up. (Luke Hauser, "mixed")

The most notable feature of these explanations is that half the women mention their early ignorance of lesbian existence. The discovery of lesbianism (usually through meeting women who identified as lesbians) was an important feature of these stories of discontinuity. It wasn't just that they could now put a name on their homosexuality, or that they could now see that there were others like them. Rather, the feelings came up only after these women discovered the possibility of lesbianism; the experience is much like that of many "chosen" lesbians, but interpreted differently. In the "chosen" account, involvement with feminism enabled the respondent to become a lesbian. In the "mixed" account, as illustrated in the quotations below, feminism enabled the respondent to realize she already was one.

> When I was nineteen I became friends with a woman who was a lesbian, but I didn't even know what it *was*. I had no idea that this existed, and I was fascinated to understand this. I decided to do a sociology paper on female homosexuality so I started reading everything I could. And as I was reading stuff like *Lesbian/Woman* and *Our Bodies, Ourselves,* I started to think that that was me. I could relate to it, several of the things that people said. And it got me real scared. (Katie Lee, "mixed")

> When I was in high school National Gay Task Force came and did a spiel. This was in '69, '70. And they were all excited about being gay and I didn't know what that was all about. Now I realize that was really like a seed, early, very early on. And later, in grad school, I learned that one of my sister's best friends was a lesbian. She lived in a notorious lesbian house at college and I went to visit. I stayed with them. And they were real nice women, I thought. And I thought, "Oh, gosh, I'm attracted to them, too." (Ruth Chang, "mixed")

Almost none of the men were unaware of male homosexuality in a parallel fashion; their stories of discontinuity are stories of denial and repression.

Finally, one woman's story of continuity involves the repudiation of her earlier, "chosen" account. Suzie Gluck, a 35-year-old Jewish woman from Brooklyn, came out in a feminist context, and at that time would have sounded much like the women I interviewed who gave the feminist "chosen" account. But over time, Suzie replaced that account with a "mixed" one.

> Well, it felt I think initially like a choice I was making. But then, the more time went on it felt like something I was really discovering about myself. I thought at the time that I didn't want to be straight, that I wanted to be a lesbian. But looking back I realize now that it was really more accepting who I was.

In the seventeen years between her coming out and the time of our interview, Suzie had earned a master's degree in social work and embarked on a career as a therapist serving a lesbian and gay clientele. Both endeavors would increase her exposure to the dominant account and its logic.

Although the "mixed" respondents' coming-out stories differ, with some "always knowing" of their homosexuality and some "discovering" it later on, those who experienced discontinuity cast their stories to minimize that difference. Their actual experiences of discontinuity are similar to those of the "chosen"-account respondents, but these respondents elect to use a "mixed" account, which aligns them with people who were continuously aware. Although they cannot themselves claim to have "always known," they do claim that the underlying reality of a homosexual orientation was "always there." The discontinuity, then, is for them only in the state of knowing. The state of being, conceived as an entirely separate realm, is continuous. "mixed"-account respondents' experiences of continuity and discontinuity do not fall somewhere between those of the "determined" and "chosen" groups, nor do they combine them. The respondents who offer the "mixed" account recall continuity (like the "determined" group) or discontinuity (like the "chosen" group). Their experiences overlap the other two account groups, but they use an account that covers both kinds of experience, uniting them under the umbrella of a single account.

A similar pattern occurs in the distribution of all sorts of experiences among the "mixed"-account respondents. Some resemble those who offer the "determined" account, while others resemble those who offer the "chosen" account. The "mixed" group includes, for example, individuals whose childhood gender conduct ranges from gender-crossing to gender-typical. About half the men of the "mixed" account group identified their childhood gender conduct as being like other boys their age.

> I had a very, quote, normal childhood. Nothing out of the ordinary. I remember rocking horses, and playing with trucks and guns. I didn't play sports, but none of my friends did either. I was in Cub Scouts, then Boy Scouts. I remember if I got into fights I would never cry. If I lost I was just cold, like nothing had happened. I would never show emotions. (Sam Broome)

> I always knew I liked guys. But I didn't—, there was a young kid on our block that was very effeminate, you know, and everybody was, "This guy's gonna grow up to be a faggot." I wasn't like that, I didn't talk like him. I didn't know where he picked those habits up from. (Darren Walker)

The other half of the "mixed" men said that as children they were "effeminate" or "sissy." Most of these men treated that as an early sign of homosexual orientation.

> It was clearly from a real early stage. I was sort of a sissy boy, not particularly athletic. So in the way that kids knew things, I knew it just in myself. Then as my mind started kicking, around ten or something, I remember reading books about homosexuality. (Al Davis)

> Being gay had been part of my subconscious being all my life. Being five years old, and not knowing what these crushes on these other boys were, and wishing I would wake up in the morning and be a girl. (Dwight Russell)

When these men recall a childhood of gender-crossing behavior, they are recalling the gap between their behavior and the local class- and ethnicity-specific expectations for heterosexual males. Their behavior may have conformed nicely to local expectations for homosexual males. For a few men who offer the "mixed" account, sissiness was not so much a matter of breaking the rules for heterosexual male behavior as a matter of following the rules for homosexual male behavior as they understood them. They see their effeminate behavior as an outcome of a gay identity, rather than as an *a priori* indicator of a homosexual orientation. Billy Fine, a 30-year-old white bartender, tells how he became more feminine after, and because, he came out.

> I was doing construction work at the time and I had a muscular body. Lots of people told me I was handsome. And when I first started coming to the gay bars, I met a lot of men that were sex changes or drag queens and somehow I thought that that's what being out and being gay meant. So I started wearing lots of eye makeup and jewelry, and one of the bartenders said to me, "Billy, you don't have to do that to be a gay man." And it was such a freeing experience that I didn't have to be something that I wasn't.

Unlike the term "sissy," the assignation "tomboy" is not entirely insulting. The young girl who aspires to boyish pursuits earns a begrudged respect, for those pursuits are considered superior by boys and girls alike (see Schur, 1984). Although like the men, about half of the "mixed"-account women engaged in gender-crossing behavior as children, there is a qualitative difference in the meaning assigned to it. Some claim childhood tomboyism as early evidence of homosexual orientation.

> In grade school I suppose I was the stereotypical model, in the sense that I was very athletic, played tackle football with the boys, and all

that sort of thing. I enjoyed that more than doing what girls did at that age. Everyone called me a tomboy. (Kate Hargrove)

But claiming a tomboy past is also claiming evidence of characteristics that are valued in many lesbian communities: physical activity and athleticism, independence, and a rejection or disregard for the typical expectations of femininity. Alice Morgan, a white 25-year-old graduate student from California, points to these with some pride.

I was a tomboy. When I was little, we lived on the beach. And practically before I could walk, I could swim in that ocean. And, I don't know, I just seemed to be more aggressive in that way. I was friends with the boys on the beach, and we were all heroic (*chuckles*) in a lot of ways.

Half the women who offer the "mixed" account point out that they were tomboys, but not all use that information to indicate their innate sexual orientation. Some talk about it the same way the "chosen" account lesbians do, the way it is presented in the classic lesbian novel of the 1970s, *Rubyfruit Jungle*: as an early and intuitive understanding that much of what femininity expresses is submission.

Just over half the "mixed"-account men told of some sexual experience with women, while nearly all the "mixed"-account women had experienced some heterosexual sex. But equivalent behavior cannot be taken to carry equivalent meanings for men and women. These women's heterosexual experience may be unrelated to their accounts of choice because, for women, heterosexual experience itself is often not fully chosen. While we could assume that the gay men of the "mixed" group in some way wanted their heterosexual experiences—even if they wanted them only in response to pressure to behave heterosexually, as was often the case—we cannot make the same assumption of the "mixed"-account lesbians. Certainly, some of the encounters counted above took place because the woman desired the man sexually. Others occurred because she wanted the experience itself, perhaps to attempt to prove to herself or to others that she was straight. But some also certainly merely went along, participating in sexual encounters they would not have initiated. And even in a group of this size, some were coerced or forced. Cindy Schwartz's experience is illustrative:

He pursued me, and once I was up in his room in the dorm and we got really drunk and we ended up having sex. And I didn't want to be having sex. So I woke up in the middle of the night and realized I wasn't home, and just got up and went downstairs to my room.

So due to the current construction of heterosexuality as male dominated, heterosexual experience is nearly a constant among these lesbians. (Other researchers have also found high levels of heterosexual experience among lesbians. See Bell and Weinberg 1978; Blumstein and Schwartz 1983.)

Both the men and women of the "mixed"-account group were less likely to have been romantically involved in a heterosexual relationship than to have experienced heterosexual sex, with more women than men recalling such relationships. Most "mixed"-account women had been emotionally involved with a man, and about half of the "mixed"-account men had been involved with a woman. Some of those relationships had been serious; two men and five women had been married or long-term cohabitators. Both of the men knew they were gay before they married, and both told their wives.

> I told my wife about it before we got married. And made it clear to her at the time that I was not unhappy with the situation, and it would not interfere with marital fidelity. It never did. It seemed to me that she was willing to accept me as what we thought at that time would be a life partner. And we sincerely meant it when we said, "Till death us do part," and we did our damnedest to make it last. (Walt Richardson)

> She knew from the beginning, and that was probably a mistake, because she was ever aware when I was watching other people, men. And felt very threatened by it. But I tried to do what I should. I thought about her, and concentrated on her and her body, in the experiences I was having with her. And we got married. Within two or three years, I was having to revert to homosexual fantasies in order to perform. (Morton Phelps)

Two of the married women, Cathy Saunders and Celia Daugherty, whose stories are discussed above, also had identified themselves as lesbians before they married, but had come to believe they were no longer. The remaining three women did not think of themselves as gay when they married or moved in with a man. Cindy Schwartz, a white 32-year-old artist from Massachusetts who works as a carpenter, was married for five years.

> I met him in a class, and I was really attracted to him. So I pursued him, really. I had to work really hard on him, because I wasn't his usual type. We moved in together, and got married in about a year.

Another two women, one each from the "mixed" and "chosen" groups, were involved with a man at the time of the interview. They account for these anomalous relationships in surprising terms. Leah Rosenthal, a 21-year-old manager of a family business, was married when we met, having wed to fulfill the expectations of her very strict Orthodox Jewish parents.

> When I first started thinking I was a lesbian, I thought, "Maybe I'm just afraid to get married." But now I'm married, and I am sure I prefer women. My therapist says that lesbianism is childish, that it's immature, and I sort of agree. But I don't care. I told him, "Then I'll stay a child."

Leah is frightened by the prospect of being alienated from her family and her religious community; nonetheless, she does see her relationship with her husband as at odds with what she really wants, which is to be with women.[10]

In contrast, Kate Hargrove, a 27-year-old magazine editor from a white, working-class, Catholic family, is currently involved in a voluntary relationship with a man. Although compulsory heterosexuality is certainly a reality that diminishes the extent to which Kate's relationship with a man can be called a choice, her situation is quite different from Leah's: Kate's family did not directly pressure her to enter this relationship, and in fact are unaware of it. She came out eight years ago, and her current heterosexual involvement does not seem to alter her lesbian identity.

> I met him through friends and he is perfectly aware of my background, but we just get along very well and it's very comfortable. And I don't think it's ever going to—I *know* that it's not going to ever be anything that will have the emotional significance that a relationship with a woman could have for me. I think we basically have a very nice friendship that also has this other sexual element at the moment and I think eventually we'll have to lose that and go back to a friendship. There was a point at which I thought perhaps it might develop more than it had, but I think if that was going to happen it would already have happened.

Leah, who is in a marriage that she entered under rather coercive circumstances, thinks of herself as lesbian by choice, while Kate, who is involved in a heterosexual relationship that she chose, considers her lesbianism to be an innate, unchosen orientation. Common-sense reasoning would predict the opposite: Leah is a real lesbian, whose current circumstances are at odds with her true identity. Kate, on the other hand, must really be bisexual, since she chose her heterosexual affiliation more freely. Apparently, there are reasons for claiming to have chosen or not chosen to be a lesbian that surpass the fit between that claim and one's personal history.

But Leah and Kate are exceptional; most discuss their (past) relationships with men in ways that are consistent with their identity account. In the examples below, Cathy Saunders, whose account is of the "mixed" type, explains her ten-year heterosexual relationship in terms of her lesbianism. Sara Pritchard, of the "chosen" group, does not offer such an explanation, allowing the apparent contradiction between that experience and her current lesbianism to stand.

That's what John was all about, was giving it a try. In giving it a try, we developed a very strong relationship. (Cathy Saunders, "mixed")

When we split, it was not for lack of love. I just had to get out on my own. (Sara Pritchard, "chosen")

In general, "chosen"-account respondents tend to embrace the contradiction between their past heterosexual experience and their current lesbian identities, and "mixed"-account respondents tend to explain it in a way that supports a belief in a continuous underlying homosexual orientation.

A final note on the gender of sexual partners: Barbara Linders, a white 25-year-old artist who works in a bookstore, is currently in a serious relationship with a pre-operative male-to-female transsexual. They clearly consider themselves a lesbian couple, and have been hurt and surprised when they have been rejected by individual lesbians and lesbian organizations. To Barbara, who offers the "mixed" account, her lover *is* a woman in every sense that matters:

VW: Did you ever think of yourself as bisexual?
BL: No, I never could really picture myself being with a man. My lover's a different case; it doesn't really matter what her body's like. I really think she's a woman inside, and that makes a difference.

Most respondents, and the structure of the interview itself, take the gender distinction between men and women for granted, and we shared an implicit definition of whom we included in the term, "woman." Barbara's relationship brings up questions that are beyond the scope of this study, but it does highlight the fact that one may define an erotic relationship between a "biological female" and a "biological male" as lesbian.

Perhaps not surprisingly, given the relatively high incidence of heterosexual experience, significant minorities of both the men and women of the "mixed" group report that they had once considered themselves bisexual. For some, that bisexual identification was a very brief stage:

I remember when my mother found out she said, "Well, at *least* consider yourself bisexual." At first I thought it would be a good cop-out so that I wouldn't be gay, but then I realized that I couldn't do that. (Patty Irving)

It's a pattern. First you say, "Maybe I'm not gay. I could change myself." And then I said to myself, "Maybe I'm bisexual," that that's the time I started to get really involved with the gay-youth group. But later, I began to accept myself, to say, "I am gay." (Thomas Labadan)

Others considered themselves bisexual for years:

> I think originally I thought I was bisexual. Actually, it was hard for me
> to accept the word "lesbian." It wasn't being with a woman that
> scared me, it was the not being with men.... I think at one point
> when I was sixteen, I walked into my shrink's office and said, "Listen,
> I'm not bisexual. I'm definitely gay." (Paula Weiss)

A few respondents of the "mixed" group, two women and two men, identify themselves as bisexual, at the same time that they describe themselves as gay or lesbian.

> I would say that I'm probably bisexual, but more of a lesbian, and I def-
> initely like to identify myself as a lesbian, and not as bisexual. (Sharon
> Halpern)

> In a way I still think of myself as bisexual, but I definitely consider
> myself gay. I don't think there's a lot of support on either side for
> being bisexual. That's really lacking. But I have made a commitment to
> my relationship at present, and it's important to me within this rela-
> tionship to consider myself gay. (Dwight Russell)

A few more express that in some way they are gay without being exclusively homosexual, although they do not use the word bisexual.

> I said I identify myself as gay, but I don't mean to imply that there
> were never women in my life. There have always been. And hopefully
> always will be. And it's not something that most people understand,
> nor do I really care at this point. (Russ Kaplan)

> VW: Did you ever think of yourself as bisexual?
> BF: No, although I have a son, and I've been with many women. I
>   totally accepted my homosexuality at a very young age, and in
>   addition to that, I knew that I could also have sex with women.
>   (Billy Fine)

> I have feelings toward men, and they're very unresolved, and there are
> a lot of question marks there. I am not willing to pursue them. There
> are a lot of issues to be dealt with, and one of them is AIDS. (Claire
> Williams)

When members of the "mixed"-account group speak of bisexuality as a temporary and incorrect self-concept, they maintain the existence of a consistent and true homosexual orientation even in the face of their sometimes considerable heterosexual experience. Some of those who offer the "chosen" account had less heterosexual experience than some of the "mixed" group. "Mixed" and "chosen" respondents' experiences with bisexual identification overlap; some of the "mixed" respondents embrace an underlying bisexuality, while a few "chosen" respondents relegate the concept to their pasts. Clearly, feeling that one is at least somewhat sexually and/or emotionally attracted toward the other gender does not necessarily lead one to claim the "chosen" account. But it does seem to be difficult to believe that one exercised complete choice in the absence of any heterosexual attraction in the present or past; all the respondents who describe this pattern offer either the "determined" or the "mixed" account.

A pattern emerges whereby the "mixed" group's range of experiences, behaviors, and self-concepts overlap those of the "chosen" and "determined" groups. Some grew up gay; others became homosexual later, experiencing a discovery. Some were typically gendered; others were tomboys and sissies; some had extensive heterosexual experience, some little or none. Some never thought of themselves as bisexual, some once did, and a few still do.

Over half of the "mixed"-account women came out over the course of the 1980s, at a median age of 20. The vast majority of the "mixed"-account men are part of the post-Stonewall generation; they came out at a median age of 19. A good number came out in earlier years, and at younger ages. Most are involved in gay and/or lesbian community life, though some lead very private lives, and a few are isolated from other gay men and lesbians. Some of the "mixed" group came out in relatively isolated contexts; most of these adopted a gay identity as children, and most are men. Half of the women came out after first getting to know other lesbians, and a very few came out in a feminist context, but did not end up adopting a "chosen" account, as did most of the women who came out in the context of the women's movement.

Class, Race, and Ethnicity

Neither religious background nor race is related to variations in the choice dimension of lesbian and gay accounts. This is not to indicate, of course, that homosexuality is experienced the same regardless of ethnicity. The Jews and people of color I interviewed talked about the various ways that their ethnic, religious, and sexual identities are related, while the Christian Euro-Americans treated these as generic. Many of the latter, the men in particular, experienced their homosexuality as their central, because their only stigmatized, identity.

> Being gay is my whole life. When I meet people, even if they're not physically attractive, my reactions to them are always as a gay person.

You view the whole world through gay eyes. A gay person, down the line. (William Sloan, "determined")

I am a lesbian; it's really what I am. It's real important to me. (Mara Pettinelli, "mixed")

Being a lesbian seems key to me right now. I don't know if that's because I haven't been out very long, you know. I don't know if that's something that changes. But it's tied in with my identity, pretty strongly. (Karen McNally, "mixed")

Some wanted to think of themselves as universally human or uniquely individual, and thought of their homosexual identity as relatively incidental.

VW: How big a part of your sense of who you are is being a lesbian?
TB: About thirty percent. (*We laugh.*) I don't know, sometimes it's a lot, depending on what's happening. Sometimes it's nothing. I'm just myself. (Terry Breiner, "determined")

In some respects being gay is very incidental. When I'm in class, I'm certainly not gay. When I'm at work I'm not. My total life is other things. It certainly is not central. I don't find it any more a part of me than when I thought of myself as straight, or when I thought of myself as bisexual. (Edward Porter, "chosen")

You know, as a human being it really isn't that big of a deal. I have the same feelings and all as anyone else. So, my sense of who I am? It just depends on what angle you're looking at me from. I'm sure if you look from a political viewpoint, it makes a lot of difference. But if you're looking at me from just a human viewpoint, it doesn't make any difference. (Rhonda Barker, "determined")

Only one person of color spoke in such terms.

A lot of the time, I forget that I'm gay. I'm a different one. To tell you the truth, I forget that I'm black sometimes too. (Lois Hayes, "chosen")

Some of the white Christian lesbians identify strongly as women as well.

It's hard for me to draw a line. I mean, I'm a human being first. Probably a woman second, and I'm a lesbian third. It is a big effect on my life in some ways. I think I have different perspectives than a straight woman. (Alice Morgan, "mixed")

It's a big part of my identity, absolutely. It's really hard for me to sepa-rate who I am as a lesbian and who I am as a feminist and who I am period into different categories. It's all one big picture. (Mary Behnke, "chosen")

Not many of the women specifically mentioned their gender as a central part of their identity, in the way that Alice and Mary do, but because the term lesbian is gender-specific, they are not forced to distinguish their identities. If gay were the only term available, they would be forced to specify their gender identity, just as the ethnic nonspecificity of the terms gay and lesbian force people of color to refer to their ethnic and sexual identities with separate terms, and allow white gay men and lesbians of dominant religions and ethnicities to think of their particu-lar experience of homosexuality as universal.

Most of the African-American, Latino, Asian-American and Jewish respon-dents spoke of identity in complex terms. Some mentioned the difficulty of maintaining both a gay and an ethnic identity when their ethnic communities are homophobic or heterosexist.

I identify with my religion, I consider myself a Jew. But I'm not prac-ticing, because there's a lot in the religion that goes against my think-ing. Basically because homosexuality is a sin in their thinking. (Sol Davidoff, "mixed")

My father's always saying, "If you give me just one grandchild I'll die peacefully," you know, and I don't say anything at all. I don't know, in the Hispanic culture, you have to have children. (Gary Perez, "mixed")

It's heavy for Latins to be accepted as a lesbian. It is heavy, and I do keep in my closet. Not with my family, but with their friends. In the neighborhood where I come from, you have to be very cool about that. 'Cause they could gang up on me or something. I always say there's a time and place for everything. You want to be gay, act like a dyke, whatever? Go the Village, go to a club. (Jessica Padilla, "mixed")

Others emphasize the problem of racism in gay communities dominated by whites.

Racism doesn't just disappear because your brother over there is gay also. He can be just as racist as someone who isn't. I know white guys who only date black guys, other white guys don't turn them on. But then, what turns them on about blacks is a very sexual, physical kind of thing, and on any other level, they don't want to deal with them. (Darren Walker, "mixed")

The women's center at school was all white. More than racism, it was like an instant expert kind of thing. "Yeah, tell us about what it's like to be a person of color! Please, we want this information from you." (Rosa Velez, "chosen")

Some speak of the pressure to identify primarily as one or the other, and particularly to proclaim a single political allegiance.

Every single one of the movements I've been in have asked me to prioritize. In the beginning, I would say, "I'm Puerto Rican first and lesbian second." Then I went through a phase of saying, "I'm lesbian first and then I'm Puerto Rican." (Lucinda Alomar, "mixed")

I once said, I don't know if I still believe it, that by itself, if one had to rank oppressions, being gay was probably more oppressive than being black, if one separated race from class. (Maurice Raymond, "mixed")

A very few still rank their multiple identities, in the way that Maurice and Lucinda once did.

I always say, and I come up against arguments about this every time I say it, but I now say that I consider myself gay first and black second. And a lot of people, a lot of black people, a lot of white people, figure that I'm not in tune with myself. I am so gay-identified nowadays that I wear it as a banner, and it's important for me to do that. (Malcolm Wilson, "determined")

VW: How big a part of you is being a lesbian?
DR: I think that my eyes are filtered through a big "L." (*We laugh.*) It's a really big, big part of me.
VW: What about your ethnicity?
DR: I never paid to much attention to that, really. (Diane Rivera, "chosen")

But most were committed to resisting the pressure to fragment their identities, to separate them and commit politically to one over the others.

When I was traveling, I felt like a Jewish New Yorker. And somehow like the lesbian stuff and the New Yorker stuff and the Jewish stuff all felt like a difference and I wanted to see whether it would tie together or not. I wanted to find a Jewish lesbian group. Being a lesbian is important as long as it's not like, the only thing. It's important to me to integrate my solidarity with other things that aren't mainstream. (Libby Markowitz, "chosen")

Now it's not necessary that I have to prioritize being lesbian and Puerto Rican. You don't have to make a choice, you just have to create your own community, which is what our group does. We're Latina, we're lesbians, all of us work in some manner or another with straight struggles. Housing, or whatever it is, but we have this home group. Our identity is there. (Lucinda Alomar, "mixed")

I still have a very strong West Indian identity, which I've finally been able to integrate with the identity which I've assumed since I've been in the U.S., which is that of a black gay man. (Maurice Raymond, "mixed")

It's not a matter of which thing I'm going to pick. Class, race, sex, we're all in here together, all 220 pounds of us. It's all very intertwined for me; all three of us wake up together in the morning. (Adrienne DuBois, "chosen")

As these quotations demonstrate, those respondents who identified with their ethnicity as well as their homosexuality talked about identity in complex terms. Most of these comments came up when I asked respondents how important being gay is to their sense who they are; some also were prompted by questions about family, politics, and the day-to-day experience of oppression. But none of the discussions excerpted above arose during conversations about choice and continuity, the central concerns of this book. Race and ethnicity matter enormously in the individual's experience of homosexuality, whether it operates to heighten the visibility of that identity, as the unquestioned nature of membership in dominant ethnic groups does, or whether it operates to create a complex web of group identifications. But, in the contemporary United States it does not seem to shape one's sense of choosing or not choosing to be gay.

Similarly, an individual's class background—i.e., the class of her or his parents—is not related to account type. Respondents' economic backgrounds range from poor to upper class, with the bulk of the respondents from middle- and working-class families. Roughly half the respondents of each account group grew up in working class or poor families, the remainder in the middle, upper-middle, and upper classes, a relationship that holds for both genders.

The effects of current class, however, seem to be gender-related. Among the men, the small "determined" account group contains a significantly larger proportion of higher-class respondents than the other two groups. The overall income level of the "determined" group is high, and includes two men who report yearly incomes over $80,000, while among the 28 respondents in the remainder of the sample, only one has an income over $50,000. All five of the "determined" respondents work in managerial, technical, or professional occupations.

Technically, the same is true of the "chosen" group. But there are three students in that group, and two self-employed freelancers. So although some of them have relatively high incomes and high-status occupations, only one holds a traditional fulltime job. As we saw above, these men tend to be isolated from gay community life; their occupational patterns add to this to suggest that they tend toward marginal and/or isolated lifestyles.

It is more difficult to measure class differences among the lesbian respondents because ordinary definitions of class do not capture the various distinctions of income, occupation, and education present in this sample. As critics have noted, sociological conceptions of class do not fit women's experiences well; with lesbians the problem is even more pronounced. Lesbians are both forbidden access to legitimated family forms (most notably by the prohibition on same-sex marriage), and freed from conventional female family roles (only one woman in this group has children). They also lack access to a man's typically higher income and do not derive their class position through marriage. As such, the employment experiences of lesbians and heterosexual women probably differ more than those of gay and straight men. Among the 39 lesbians in this sample, current class is not significantly related to account type. There are upwardly and downwardly mobile, economically marginal and fully employed respondents in all three groups. Ettore's (1980) finding that lesbians who claim choice have fewer "stakes in the system" than those who claim an unchosen orientation is not replicated here.

Choosing a Story

Respondents' accounts do not merely recount their experiences; they are stories told to fit those experiences into a coherent, conventionalized story. The largest group of respondents, those who use the "mixed" account to speak for themselves and others, is an amalgam of individuals whose personal histories of love, sex, and gender differ profoundly. Many "mixed"-account respondents always knew they were gay, never thought they were or could be bisexual, have little heterosexual experience, and were seen as atypical children for their gender; they *could* use the "determined" account, but they don't. Other "mixed" respondents changed their identity from heterosexual to homosexual, thought of themselves as bisexual (or perhaps still do), have a good deal of heterosexual experience, which they may have enjoyed, and were not considered tomboys or sissies; they *could* tell their stories using the "chosen" account, but they do not. Most respondents, whatever their experience, utilize the "mixed" account. As the dominant account, it assimilates alternatives; there is no experience it cannot be used to explain. That is, in fact, the point of its appeal.

The "chosen" and "determined" account are less robust; if this sample included only those who use one of these two accounts, my conclusions about the relationship between experience and account would be different, for the two groups are distinguished on nearly every measure: heterosexual experience, bisexual identification, childhood gender behavior, age at coming out. But these are not the only two account types, so the pattern is more complex. For example, though nearly all "determined" respondents recall continuous awareness of their homosexuality, the reverse is not true; not all respondents who recall continuity offer the "determined" account. Similarly, while nearly everyone who offers the "chosen" account experienced discontinuity, not everyone with a discontinuous identity history offers the "chosen" account. Most respondents, whatever their experience of identity continuity, use the "mixed" account. Respondents want to use it, and so they are willing to do the cognitive and emotional work to fit their experience to its contours.

Nowhere is this more evident than when many "mixed"-account respondents retrospectively interpret their pasts in order to create narrative continuity in the face of a discontinuous history. "I was always gay but didn't know it" is a recognizable claim that is consistent with commonsense understandings of sexual orientation. Its user is welcomed under the umbrella of the dominant account. In contrast, Henry Yount's claim that he chose to be gay without being aware of doing so is idiosyncratic, and would probably be rejected by most listeners.

Such a claim reaches few ears. For perhaps the most distinguishing characteristic of the men who use the "chosen" account is that they are relatively isolated from gay community life. They have had few or no lovers or gay friends. Some state that they are "basically bisexual," but some who offer the "mixed" account make that claim as well. Each of these six men *could* use the "mixed" account, could make it fit their experiences as well as it fits many other men's. But they don't use it because they are not a part of the community whose story the "mixed" account tells. They have developed their accounts in relative isolation; they even use them as a symbolic barrier that marks their alienation from other gay men, as Henry Yount does below.

> I began to think a lot about choice, and why we're not permitted to see it as a choice, and why it's not talked about as a choice. If you ask most homosexuals, they'll say, "No, I didn't have a choice. I was born this way."

For most respondents, accounts mark their similarity to others, not their distance from them. This is particularly so for respondents who use the "mixed" account, for they tell not only a shared story but in fact the only story, the one that explains how it is for everyone. By using the "mixed" account in one's personal narrative, an individual both draws upon and contributes to a collective discourse that is a piece of the process of sexuality formation. Like Omi and Winant's concept of "racial formation," sexual formation is "the historical process by which [sexual] categories are created, inhabited, transformed, and destroyed" (1994: 55). Accounts are the site of a dynamic interaction between collective and individual social processes that create homosexuality—and by extension heterosexuality—as categories.

The collective account also aims to neutralize stigma and argue for legitimacy. It portrays homosexuality as an essential and immutable characteristic, and at the same time recognizes the political importance of choosing to come out—to one's self, to friends and family, to a public. We do not choose to be gay, but we can, do, and must choose to come out. The account tells the story of a collective strategy. That strategy was the brainchild of the post-Stonewall generation, for whom "come out, come out, wherever you are" was an imperative. And among the men in this sample it is those respondents who came out before 1969 who are most likely to hold to an account other than the dominant one. The men who use the dominant account, on the other hand, nearly all came out after Stonewall, and are generally well integrated into gay community life.

That community life was relatively sex-segregated throughout the 1970s, due as much to the explosive growth of urban gay male ghettoes (Levine 1979) as to the separatism of lesbian-feminism. As such, gay male and lesbian identity accounts may have converged less in the 1970s than they did a decade later. Among the "mixed"-account lesbians in this sample, two thirds came out during the 1980s, the years when joint gay-lesbian organizations multiplied under the pressure of AIDS and the right-wing backlash, and when lesbian-feminism lost its central place in lesbian culture (Stein 1992).

The "determined"-account group is so small in this sample that it is difficult to analyze. The men who offer this account are well integrated into gay community life, and tend to be older and wealthier than the men who use the "mixed" account. But like the "mixed"-account men, they assume that theirs is the account that speaks for everyone. In their eyes, their account is the dominant account, and clearly the distinction between the "determined" and "mixed" accounts is slight compared to the gulf dividing the "chosen" account from the other two. The "determined"-account women, on the other hand, do not assume that theirs is the dominant account. Because "chosen" accounts are more viable, and more common, for lesbians than for gay men, these women must be aware that they don't speak for everyone.

The four women whose "chosen" account was based on an underlying bisexual orientation resembled the "chosen"-account men in their tendency to be only tangentially connected to lesbian community life; they offer an account that, at the time these interviews took place, lacked the authority of a collective experience. Since that time many women and men have asserted a bisexual identity and have successfully pressed for recognition in lesbian and gay-movement organizations, particularly on college campuses. As we have seen, many "chosen" and "mixed" respondents told me that their underlying, basic, or technical orientations were bisexual; perhaps some of them today identify as bisexual rather than lesbian or gay. But such an outcome is by no means certain, for I do not see these individuals as bisexuals waiting for the chance to speak the truth. Identities have proliferated, not simply become more and more accurate.

If, in 1988, the bisexual version of the "chosen" account remained an individual story, the feminist "chosen" account was clearly a collective one; all of the women who use it came out in a feminist context of one sort or another. (I do not posit that exposure to feminism "produces" lesbian-feminists; a few "mixed"-account respondents also came out in a feminist context but do not use the "chosen" account.) The feminist context was the immediate source of their account, but the questions remain of why they ever were drawn to it, why they ever made it work for them.

I have identified some of the interpretive work that those who use the "mixed" account perform to make their experiences fit it. What do the lesbian-feminists who use a "chosen" account do to maintain it as truth? This process is less visible than the "mixed"-account respondents' process. Although some of the "chosen" account respondents are selectively interpreting their pasts when they make a point of stating that they had enjoyed sex with men (a few offer this information within their first statements in the interview), they never reinterpret their pasts to reach this point.

I have thus far left the feminist "chosen" account relatively intact, giving the appearance of assumed truth. I have certainly paid more attention to the dominant account, not to claim that it is false, but to determine why it is the preferred truth among many possible ones. The alternative accounts, on the other hand, already appear to be untrue, and those who use them are already seen as false lesbians. Nonetheless, in the next chapter I will unravel some of the functions of the lesbian-feminist "chosen" account. As we shall see, it distinguishes lesbians from gay men and provides a political link to heterosexual women, providing good reason—aside from accuracy—to utilize this account.

While many "mixed"-account respondents have life histories that could easily fit a "determined" account, and many have histories that could easily fit a "chosen" account, gender complicates the picture. If the women who use the "mixed" account were to use another, most would best fit their stories to a "chosen" account. And if the "mixed" account men were to switch accounts, it would most likely be to a "determined" account. Put another way, those variables that tend to differentiate "determined"- from "chosen"-account respondents also tend to differentiate the gay men from the lesbians. In both pairings, the latter group is more likely to have experienced discontinuity of sexual identity, and to have more heterosexual experience. So the "mixed" account assimilates not only varying experiences but different genders as well; it creates the appearance of similarity between lesbians and gay men. Walt describes that appearance perfectly:

> Gay men and lesbians are simply two sides of exactly the same coin. (Walt Richardson)

It's a similarity that is central to the representation of homosexuality as a sexual orientation that floats free from gender rather than a gender inversion. As Chauncey (1982–83) has persuasively argued, the "homosexuality" concept fully replaced the "gender-inversion" concept only when it was eventually applied to women as well as men. But applying it to women requires the retrospective interpretation of their pasts, a vigorous effort made less often by men. So it is women who perform the lion's share of the cognitive and emotional labor that keeps the dominant account in place. The next chapter will argue that the dominant account does more for and requires less of men than of women.

Notes

1. Ponse (1978) distinguishes between lesbians whose identity history is continuous, whom she calls "primary," and those whose identity histories are discontinuous. The latter characterizes the lesbians whose identities Ponse terms "elective," a term which tends to conflate choice and continuity. Here I am building on Ponse's insights by distinguishing between these.

2. The process of taking on a heterosexual identity is not parallel to the process of taking on a lesbian or gay identity. Most people who identify as straight never "decided" on that identity, or "discovered" that orientation, or "admitted" those desires. It is entirely possible to adopt a heterosexual identity as a default, simply by allowing the nearly universal assumption of heterosexuality to settle upon one.

3. I allowed respondents to define "sexual experience" for themselves. When they talked about heterosexual experience, they were nearly always referring to intercourse, which is the act that "counts" as sex in the popular conception.

4. A third cohort, those men who came out after the beginning of the AIDS epidemic, has now passed its first decade. At the time of these interviews, it was nascent.

5. I use the term "gay community life" instead of "gay community" to underline the point that there are many communities, and many ways to be involved in them.

6. Chi-square 6.18, dof = 2, $p < .05$. Because this sample is not randomly selected, I am not using this statistic to estimate probability, but simply as a convenient device for determining which relationships I will treat as noteworthy.

7. Chi-square 12.55, dof = 2, $p<.01$

8. Among lesbians the distinction between those who "grew up gay" and those who didn't is commonly recognized. One researcher demonstrates that this form of difference is live enough to be a significant piece of relationship dynamics, and she even suggests that continuous and discontinuous lesbians tend to be drawn to one another (Burch 1993).

9. Ponse (1978) calls the process "biographical reconstruction."

10. It was clearly a difficult time for her, and I have often wondered where she is now. After our interview, we talked casually for a while and I told her that I, too, had come out when I was married and that everything had eventually worked out. She rose immediately from her chair and bolted from the room, scarcely saying goodbye. I did not hear from her again.

five

Difference and Dominance: Gendered Identity Accounts

As previous chapters have demonstrated, the distinction between the "determined" and "mixed" accounts is largely a matter of degree; it is certainly not as ideologically loaded as the distinction between then and the "chosen" account. For the purposes of the present chapter, then, I will seldom refer separately to the "determined" account, but will include the elements shared by it and the "mixed" account in the term "dominant account." That dominant account of gay identity achieves a unity of the homosexual across genders the way the term "gay" does, by centering gay male, and marginalizing lesbian, experience. Lesbians, compared to gay men, are less inclined to believe they were born gay, are more likely to have various forms of heterosexual experience and/or identity over the course of their lives, and are more apt to claim that their sexual preference is chosen. Given what accounts do, which is to connect the individual with the collective as part of a political strategy, why are lesbians more likely than gay men to use a "chosen" account?[1] Because lesbians struggle with both sexism and heterosexism, lesbian identity accounts must serve complex and competing purposes.

In some sense the answer is evident: Lesbians are more likely than gay men to claim to have chosen their sexual preference because they have available to them, in lesbian-feminism, an articulate and fully formulated group account the likes of which is unavailable to men. As we have seen, the women who use the feminist "chosen" account are well integrated into lesbian community life; they may be a numerical minority among lesbians, but they are a recognized and organized minority. In contrast, the women who use a bisexual "chosen" account, and all the "chosen"-account men, tend to be more isolated; some could even be described as loners. Individuals of both genders who offered accounts for which there is no community of discourse tend to be isolated, in what is probably a relationship of two-way causality. Like the dominant account, a lesbian-feminist account provides a narrative that is useful to those who plug their personal stories into it. It provides an alternative to the dominant account.

This answer, however, only refocuses the question. The lesbian-feminist notion that one could or should choose lesbianism for political reasons was not an inevitable development of feminism. Even if it were a logical outcome of the belief that the personal is political, logical inevitability hardly insures social and political success. The women who formulated the tenets of lesbian-feminism were part of a cohort who were making and acting upon their own choices. Whether or not lesbian-feminism was logically inevitable, the question remains: Why do lesbians have available to them two contrasting accounts regarding choice while gay men have only one?

As I argue in Chapter Two, the mainstream gay- and lesbian- rights movement's positions on choice and related issues centers and favors a gay subject that is white and male. And as Chapters Three and Four demonstrate, those positions shape and are shaped by individuals' use of the dominant account. In short, the dominant account allows gay men to maintain their claim on male privilege. The legitimacy claim founded on the premise that an essential difference in sexual orientation—and only that—distinguishes heterosexuals from homosexuals leaves other categories of dominance and subordination unchallenged. The claim to a right to be treated the same as others without regard to sexual orientation is an insufficient claim for lesbians unless gender inequality is addressed simultaneously. The prospect of reaching a status equal to heterosexuals of one's own gender promises more to gay men than to lesbians. Of course, the majority of the gay men I interviewed are sympathetic to the feminist movement, and gay men certainly are a force for change in understandings of masculinity (see Carrigan, et al., 1985). But the bid for acceptance contained in the dominant account tends away from, not toward, political engagement with gender inequality.

A small number of the men I interviewed use similar terms to criticize the mainstream movement. Maurice Raymond points to the assumption of privilege by "most white gay men."

> I think gay men have not done a much better job, pre-AIDS, of being anything less than men. Or more than men. I mean, there is a potential; I think that gayness has a radicalizing potential. But it so often fails to realize itself in most white gay men.

Two of these men were deeply committed to AIDS activism, and in 1987 were clearly forming some of the ideas of "gay nationhood" that became widespread with the birth of Queer Nation in 1990. They minimized the assimilationist implications of the dominant account; Russ Silver rejects the idea entirely.

> I have no interest in being accepted. I consider this system corrupt, and I don't want to be accepted by it. We're in this together. Faggots, junkies, women, blacks, Hispanics, Native Americans, Asians, don't you see it? Don't you see that our white male government doesn't care about us? When I say this it shocks coat-and-tie lesbians and gay men everywhere. Well, I'm sorry, folks; if you had AIDS you would know what I know: The government doesn't give a goddamn cent for a faggot's life.

For Russ, who died two years after this interview, living as a person with AIDS was a radicalizing experience, one that put him—and others who were similarly radicalized—at odds with a "coat-and-tie" movement.

Divisions among the forms of lesbian politics, like distinctions among lesbian identity accounts, are even wider. Compared to that of gay men, lesbian identity must negotiate a more difficult political course, one that must pass between the Scylla of female heterosexuality and the Charybdis of male homosexuality. Both of these more visible categories threaten to swallow lesbian existence; too close an identification with either is dangerous. As we shall see, both of the major lesbian identity accounts seek to avoid these dangers, and neither succeeds entirely.

Lesbianism is beyond the collective imagination in a society where women's sexuality is positioned as subordinate and receptive to that of men. A few of the lesbians I interviewed felt how heavily the heterosexist assumption weighs on women in particular:

> VW: So right now you're not looking to get involved with anyone?
> AB: That's scary to say, because I like being involved with women, you know. It's hard to be a lesbian and not be in a relationship, you know? (Anna Blumberg, "chosen")

> It's like, "When you're not in a relationship, are you a lesbian?" That thing. And it's like that's what I feel sometimes. You know, if I'm choosing to be celibate right now does that mean I'm going to turn into a big funky heterosexual monster all over again? [Laughs.] (Diane Rivera, "chosen")

> Now I can say I'm a lesbian, you know, because I have a lover now. Before I couldn't. (Barbara Linders)

In such an androcentric context, lesbians have made themselves visible, indeed possible, by defining themselves as adjuncts to other more powerful social groups (Whisman 1994). The "invert" of the early 20th century distinguished herself from seemingly asexual and nonthreatening "romantic friends" by emphasizing the ways she was like a (straight) man (Faderman 1991; Newton 1984; Smith-Rosenberg 1989). The "female homophile" who appeared mid-century emphasized sexual preference over gender; she shared her homosexuality with gay men (Martin and Lyon 1972). The lesbian-feminist of the 1970s emphasized her commonalities with straight women, and downplayed any she might have shared with men of any sexual identity (Johnston 1975, Rich 1980). These definitional strategies have expanded the space of lesbian possibility over the course of the twentieth century, and they continue to do so. The distinction between lesbians who do and do not claim to have chosen their sexualities enters this history, as lesbian claims about choice support different definitional strategies.

The Charybdis of Male Homosexuality

As Carol Gilligan's (1982) classic study showed, the moral reasoning of women appears faulty only when it is measured against a male standard. Similarly positioned, lesbian experience looks like a weak version of homosexuality. Surveys of large samples of lesbians and gay men (Bell and Weinberg, 1978; Blumstein and Schwartz, 1983) show that lesbians tend to have experienced more heterosexual sex than gay men, are more likely to have been married, and are more likely to experience discontinuity of sexual preference over the course of their lives. Similar patterns characterize the group of respondents I interviewed. Several of the lesbian respondents, and a few of the gay men, mention these gendered patterns.

> It seems that for most gay men, my impression is that that's something they generally tend to be aware of much younger, and I don't know why it seems to be that way, because for so many other things it's the opposite. (Kate Hargrove, "mixed")

> With lesbians, it's a different case. Usually women would go through the period of dating, and having boyfriends and going through the processes that society expects a woman to do. And maybe a lot of them would even end up getting married and having kids. And finally realizing that's not their life. (Thomas Labadan, "mixed")

How does the essentialist understanding which undergirds the dominant account handle gender differences such as these? The understanding of homosexuality as an orientation would suggest that those who experience discontinuity are somehow faulty. For if individuals are either homosexual or heterosexual, as an unchanging orientation, then the time period prior to the recognition of one's homosexuality is a period of ignorance. Individuals for whom this period is relatively longer are simply more unaware, less in touch with their underlying orientation. Nearly all the respondents, men and women, whose sexual lives were discontinuous think of it this way. As we saw in Chapter Four, their experience of identity change did not show them that they were not always homosexual; it merely showed that they were not always aware of it. As a result of that reasoning, some were ashamed of what they saw as their ignorance or denial. Men as well as women expressed such concerns; but the experience of discontinuity from which they arise is nearly twice as common among women in this sample.

> The logical progression would seem to be that by the age of ten or eleven or twelve, I would have realized that I was gay. It's possible that it was entering my mind, but that for some reason I was blocking it out or saying no, but I don't remember that. It's a question I've often had: "What happened to all those years?" (Robert Henderson, "mixed")

> I think for a long time I sort of felt something bad about myself because it took me so long to be a lesbian. I felt like, "What didn't I see? Why wasn't I more aware earlier?" I know initially I felt some embarrassment, because here I was twenty-eight or whatever. (Karen McNally, "mixed")

It's not only those who experience discontinuity who recognize these implications of the essentialist model. A few of the men who had "always known" they were gay commented upon those who had not.

> I think people are born gay. From what I know from myself, and just from talking to other people, it seems like they knew at an early age. Even the people who come out later, are kind of, I don't want to say dumb, but they just were the sort of people who were always doing what people told them to do. And they never really examined themselves. (Brent McKenna, "mixed")

> DB: Do some people think you can not know you're gay if you are?
> VW: Oh yes, I've heard people say that about their own lives. "I was always gay but I didn't know it until I was thirty." That kind of thing.
> DB: They didn't always know? I find that hard to believe. If they think so, that's their own business, but it doesn't make sense. (Dan Bartlett, "determined")

These statements are gender-neutral, but the phenomenon referred to by these men as "dumb," the experience that "doesn't make sense," is more often a feature of lesbian than gay-male experience.

Although I did not ask respondents to provide an explanation for this gendered pattern, some offered speculations on their own. Implicitly taking male sexuality as the "unrepressed" norm, they suggested that lesbian experience is different because women's sexuality is hindered by passivity, socialization, repression, or victimization. Sherry Pero's more symmetrical statement is a notable exception to this tendency to treat male behavior as "normal" or unaffected by socialization.

> You know, I think that women are repressed sexually to begin with. Gay men are repressed in other areas, emotionally. Our society forces it on us. (Sherry Pero, "mixed")

> A lot of girls really bother me, because I feel like they buy into this girl-ness. I always wonder how many women kind of lead their regular heterosexual lives, but don't really feel like that. (Diane Rivera, "chosen")

> A lot of women in school decided that women are much nicer to be around. The violence—I know someone who was raped many times, within a family, and she does not want to be around men. So in that sense, I know women who've chosen to be lesbians. (Terry Breiner, "determined")

> Is it because of conditioning? Perhaps women at very early ages are forced into a specific role that they have to play. So it could be that as adults some women, some of them blossom in a way. (Malcolm Wilson, "determined")

> A lot of that has to do with how we're enculturated and socialized. In terms of men being decision-makers about their lives, feeling like if they want to go fuck a guy, who's to say anything about it. Whereas women are more pushed into molds. (Al Davis, "mixed")

In these quotations, gay men are generic homosexuals and lesbians are a "sex-specific deviation from that allegedly univeral standard" (Bem 1993:41). It is not only within gay worlds that men are generic and women "other," to be sure; androcentrism shapes the construction of gender at the broadest level (Bem 1993, Schur 1984). But the essentialist understanding of homosexuality contained in the dominant account reinforces the pattern.

In contrast, the lesbian-feminist model portrays discontinuity between one's former heterosexual and current lesbian identities as no source of embarassment. A new lesbian-feminist's earlier life might sometimes be portrayed as a period of pre-enlightenment, rejected after the eye-opening experience of consciousness raising, but there is no suggestion that she should have known earlier, and certainly no suggestion that her experience would look more like a gay man's if it weren't distorted by her gender.

Having portrayed gay male experience as gender-neutral, the essentialist model of homosexuality informs a politics that inevitably fails to address gender inequality. Although few of the lesbians I interviewed were familiar with lesbian-feminist theory, most articulated a belief that compulsory heterosexuality oppresses women. Two-thirds of the women who were asked the question, "Do you think a lot of women would be better off as lesbians?" answered affirmatively.

> (*Chuckles.*) Yeah, I honestly do. At least in this society, right now I do. Just because I think men have so much, so far to go to catch up to women in terms of emotional strength, that yeah, I do. (Sharon Halpern, "mixed")

> Yeah, sometimes (*chuckles*). Because a lot of the women I know have horrible times with men. It's kind of strange for me to think, "Yeah, some women would be better off being lesbians," but I have thought it before. Because there's not so much of a power struggle, and women talk to each other easier. But it's not going to happen. (Rhonda Barker, "determined")

> Yes, always (*laughs*). Yes, definitely. If all the men in the world fell off the face of the earth it would be no great loss as far as I was concerned. Yes, definitely. (Katie Lee, "mixed")

> Yes, as a matter of fact I'm surprised that there aren't more lesbians, even than we know of. Because it's ridiculous what people expect of relationships with men. It's really sick. They're supposed to be so different. Women are supposed to be weak, all those things. (Tina Fiore, "chosen")

Nearly all the "chosen" respondents answered affirmatively, and half of the women who gave the "mixed" and "determined" accounts did as well, even though the very idea of such a question challenges other assumptions of the dominant account.

Men tended to respond to the question in a manner more consistent with their accounts. Three-fourths of the men who were asked a similar question about men responded negatively. Moreover, they seemed to find the question imponderable as I phrased it, and most implicitly or explicitly reframed the query in essentialist terms.

> Do you mean admitting they were gay? Because I don't think this is something where one can say, "Well, uh, I've been straight all my life

and nothing seems to work; maybe I better try being gay." I can see, "I have behaved as though I were straight all my life, and nothing has worked; maybe I better show my true colors." This is definitely a possibility. (Walt Richardson, "mixed")

No, not at all. Most people would be better off being who they are. (Billy Fine, "mixed")

No, but I do remember going through this thing of "Oh, that one's really gay. And he's really gay. And she's really gay." (Dwight Russell, "mixed")

The few men who did answer this question affirmatively were stating that the condition of marginality itself creates a depth of character.

(Chuckles.) Yeah. I think gay people right now are representing one of the most maligned and oppressed peoples. And I think they're dealing with that in a very warm and loving way. I think a lot of people, if they were in this position, would understand how they can get through life a lot easier. (Luke Hauser, "mixed")

The women claim that relationships with men are or can be oppressive to women. There are many reasons why men would not believe the reverse; and if they did believe it, there is cause to suspect that they would hesitate to say it to a female interviewer. Nonetheless, whether or not women's affirmative answers are wishful thinking, they are an example of putting aside essentialist beliefs in the process of making some connection between sexual preference and the subordination of women, an insight lacking in the dominant account. The lesbian-feminist version of the "chosen" account highlights that connection through its disregard for the boundary between hetero- and homosexuality. For many gay men, that boundary is not only acceptable, but a valuable source of legitimacy and self-esteem, as Sol Davidoff explicitly states.

I've come to the conclusion that the world is filled with four types of people. Men who love women, women who love men, men who love men, and the women who love women. And I think we all didn't really have a choice in the matter. That's really what's out there. It's not like we're all on a straight track of a train, and then some of us turn off somewhere and become gay.

The Scylla of Female Heterosexuality

Why, given its limitations, do so many lesbians continue to hold to the dominant account? Why has it not been entirely eclipsed by the lesbian-feminist account?

Certainly the dominant account's entrenchment is a factor. It appears self-evident, less an account at all than a simple statement of the obvious truth. But we cannot assume that all lesbians would use the lesbian-feminist account if it were more accessible to them. To do so would be to overlook what the dominant account actually does for women.

The lesbian-feminist account is far from perfectly satisfactory itself. It has been criticized for elitism (Zita 1981), racism (Combahee River Collective 1984), and historical inaccuracy (Ferguson 1981). But the most consistently heard criticism of lesbian-feminism has attacked its "anti-sex bias" (Alderfer, et al. 1982; Ferguson, et al. 1984; Hollibaugh and Moraga 1981; Rubin, 1981; Snitow, et al. 1983). The problem noted by these critics was partly the proclivity of groups of lesbian-feminists to join other radical feminists in political activism against pornography and sadomasochism. But more centrally, the lesbian-feminist account itself portrays lesbianism in asexual terms. For if a lesbian is a woman-identified woman who bonds with other women, then she is not a sexual outlaw who desires sex with other women. And in the early 1980s, many lesbians began to identify as the latter, and to reject the culture, politics, and identity of lesbian-feminism.

These "lesbian sex wars" were not of great concern to the women I interviewed. If few of them identified with lesbian-feminism, fewer still were familiar with the "pro-sex" critique. Nonetheless, the sex debates point to a dilemma that lesbians do face, even if they are not producing lesbian theory. When lesbians define themselves primarily as women, emphasizing the links with heterosexual women and downplaying those with gay men, they deemphasize their sexuality. And the dominant account, even though it portrays that sexuality as a lesser version of male homosexuality, does emphasize the importance of sex.

When lesbians define themselves in terms of essentialist homosexuality they define themselves by their sexual desire—no small feat in a culture that continues to characterize female sexuality in terms of how it attends, responds, or appeals to the sexuality of men. So while stepping into a conceptual category shaped by gay male experience may make lesbians appear to be incompetent homosexuals, the move is not without its advantages. In the quotations below, respondents make a claim to sexual agency through the explicit rejection of choice.

> There have been an occasional few, maybe like, younger people, that I think have chosen to live like a lesbian, live as lesbians, but I don't think they're really lesbians, and I think that eventually they'll become heterosexual. Because I don't think they have the stamina to keep going. I guess I've seen a lot of people, women in their twenties, in the bars, just flirting with their girlfriends, and um, going home with them, not always having sex, just sleeping together. (Cindy Schwartz, "mixed")

> KM: I feel like some people choose to be lesbians because it's fashionable, or because it seems like the ultimate feminist statement.

VW: So if a friend told you that she wasn't sure whether she was gay or straight, how would you help her decide?

KM: I guess I would ask her why she thought she was gay, and if she was definitely attracted to women on a sexual level, or if it was more political. (Karen McNally, "mixed")

Unlike chosen lesbians, real lesbians, according to these statements, feel a strong and specifically *sexual* desire for other women. By making that claim, these women—all of whom count themselves among the real lesbians—name their desire.

By doing so they reject a major feature of the way female sexuality is constructed. Ever forced to exchange their sexuality for something else—love, protection, money—women experience their sexual desires as more firmly in their control than do men, who are encouraged to experience their sexuality as a barely containable drive (Collins 1974, Beauvoir 1952, Firestone 1970). As such, it's not terribly surprising that lesbians are more likely than gay men to use a "chosen" account; the conventional, and heterosexual, construction of gendered sexualities would predict that very pattern. In fact, in the face of gendered division of sexual "control," what is surprising is that so many lesbians report that they *didn't* choose to be gay. That surprise—and the disjuncture it represents between what lesbians claim and what the conventional construction of female sexuality would predict—is precisely the point. When lesbians say they didn't choose to be gay they treat their sexuality as uncontrollable, and as such stake a claim to a sanctified male privilege.

Conclusion

Even if the dominant account serves gay men better than it serves lesbians, a lesbian-feminist account is not without problems of its own. We cannot assume that lesbians who use the dominant account are falsely conscious or always unaware of the alternatives. Faced with two imperfect alternatives, they choose between them. One of those alternatives is advantaged in that choice, to be sure; the dominant account has all the appeal of common sense on its side—and is far more widely known as well. But lesbians use that account, even while they are used by it.

The dominant understanding of gay identity proposes no critique of male dominance. Indeed, it actually reproduces it in the way that it casts male homosexuality as universal and lesbianism as particular. It is also a model with narrow political implications. Lacking a critique of heterosexuality, the family, and gender inequality, the movement is limited to either a nationalist or a minority-rights framework. Since it is understood that sexual preference is not chosen and cannot be changed, there is no space for talking about why one might *want* to be gay. Many lesbians do have beliefs about why one might want to be a lesbian, but they see those beliefs as out of place. They laugh at themselves even as they say that yes, they do believe many women would be better off as lesbians.

Lesbian-feminism makes that claim unapologetically, providing an alternative account that focuses on lesbian experience and links it to a larger politics of gender inequality. But lesbian-feminism achieves that link at the cost of lesbian sexuality. The dominant account, for all its problems, does define lesbianism in specifically sexual terms. By aligning lesbians with gay men, this model portrays lesbians as sexual in a way that alignment with heterosexual women fails to do.

Neither of these models provides an account of lesbianism that does everything it needs to do: treat lesbian, not generic, hetero-, or homosexual male, experience as a norm, emphasize the importance of sexuality in a lesbian identity, and include an understanding that lesbians are both akin to and different from gay men and straight women. Thus the lesbian-feminist account has neither eclipsed the dominant account nor has it disappeared. And as the next chapter's discussion of identity politics will suggest, we are mistaken to believe that we will someday arrive at the right identity account that truly represents the lesbian.

Notes

1. But to state that choice is a particularly lesbian experience is in some way to miss the larger point that *variability* is quintessentially lesbian. Lesbian sexual histories, sexual preferences, and accounts seem to vary more widely than gay men's.

six

Conclusion

Lesbian and gay accounts—of which various statements about choice are a part—are ways of entering inherently political discourses. They both create and invoke arguments that have been used to battle heterosexist cultures and institutions—and sometimes androcentric ones as well. As such these accounts function like religious testimony, the purpose of which "is not only to strengthen an individual's faith but also to build a faith of the community" (James Cone, quoted in hooks and West: 1991).

To emphasize this function is not to suggest that lesbian and gay identity accounts do nothing else. Personal narratives (of all sorts, not only sexual ones) are central to how we construct our most basic sense of self. The belief that one is who one is supposed to be may be an abdication of personal responsibility ("bad faith," in existentialist terms), but it is a very comforting one. Many respondents mentioned to me, entirely in passing, that some non-sexual features of their lives were preordained. "I was always a feminist," more than a few claimed; one said, "I always knew I'd be an architect"—in terms that vividly paralleled their claims of an innate homosexuality.[1] Individuals who understand the self as contingent can experience that as a source of pain, such as Diane Rivera expresses here:

> I tried to even make a story. I was like, "Well, what do I have to talk about?" There's no story that equals "lesbian." And I was waiting for it to, like, shine in front of my eyes. I've picked the brains of those

ones who say they knew when they were in fifth grade, you know?
[*Laughs.*] Sometimes I think, "Maybe I'll find a story that will remind
me or something will, you know, click." It would be nice to have a
story.

I have left unexplored most of the ways that individuals use narrative to create
a continuous self, in order to focus on the political functions of accounts. But a
reminder may be in order that political discourse is not the only process that
shapes lesbians' and gay men's identity accounts; personal narratives hold exis-
tential dread at bay.

The dominant account of lesbian and gay identity holds that the individual's
homosexuality is determined by factors beyond her or his control while acting
upon, accepting, and identifying with that orientation are matters of choice. This
reasoning allows a wide range of experiences to be incorporated as variations on
a single theme, reducing the apparent diversity of sexualities. It constructs a uni-
tary homosexuality even as it represents it.

Like the mainstream movement with which it dovetails, the dominant
account serves some better than others. The underlying logic of the account—
based on an understanding of male behavior as genderless, of male sexuality as
the unrepressed norm—portrays lesbians as faulty, derivative. What could be
described as the sexual flexibility of many lesbians is described instead as ignorance or lack of awareness. The lesbians who claim the dominant account for
their own must go to greater lengths than comparable gay men to make it fit their
lives, more frequently using retrospective interpretation to explain away their
pasts. They also cannot incorporate a feminist critique of compulsory heterosexuality into that model of sexual preference, even though many do hold to such a
critique in some form and do believe that lesbianism and feminism are somehow
connected.

The few gay male respondents who claim to have chosen to be gay are relatively isolated individuals who apparently could relate their past experience in the
terms of the dominant account but who choose not to do so. (Since the time of
the interviews, in 1987, these men could have explored connections to either the
bisexual or the queer movements, innovations which in some ways responded to
the felt isolation of just such individuals.) Such men are exceptional, while lesbians who hold to an alternative account are not so unusual. The lesbian-feminist
account that they use, however, de-emphasizes sexuality to such an extent that it
has not replaced the dominant account among lesbians and likely will not. As of
yet, no alternative lesbian account incorporates gender politics and sexuality.

Even while they serve political purposes, and take at least some of their con-
tent from a movement agenda, these accounts would be strange indeed if they
entirely avoided individuals' actual sexual histories. While variations of experience among the three account type groups overlap considerably—and the

"mixed" account can handle all patterns of sexual experience—it's also clear that the sexual histories of the "chosen" and "determined" groups tend in opposite directions on most variables. Members of either group could fit their experience to the "mixed" account, as we have seen, but most "determined" account respondents would appear odd claiming a "chosen" account, and vice versa. One may tell many stories about one's life, but it does not follow that one may tell any story at all. Most people make an effort to be accurate; experience does matter, and impulse and desire do vary considerably among individuals. Far from pointing to the singular experience or indicator of homosexuality, these findings suggest that, like the dominant account, the concept of homosexuality covers a wide variety of experiences and individuals. Homosexuality is a nucleus around which we cluster, not an essence that we share. Nowhere is this more clearly demonstrated than in comparisons between lesbians and gay men.

In common-sense thinking, identity is the sum total of a number of discrete categories. And so one adds "homosexual" plus "female" and arrives at "lesbian." In practice, however, many of the meanings attached to the concept of homosexuality are altered by admixture of female gender. Is homosexuality necessarily exclusive? Consistent over the individual's lifespan? Can it be chosen? Is it related to gender inequality? The usual answers to these questions would be quite different if the conceptualization of homosexuality began with lesbian experience. Then it might not work very well for many men. So the problem may not only be that the generic homosexual is assumed to be male, but that such a concept outside of its particular, gendered existence is a distortion. Rather, as Weeks has put it, "Lesbians and gay men are not two genders within one sexual category" (1985: 203).

Although this study has not been concerned with the standard etiological question ("What 'causes' homosexuality?") and has not used the kind of data that would answer it, a position on the issue is implied. Regardless of what gay men and lesbians claim in their accounts, do they all really choose to be gay? I began this work believing that many lesbians and gay men exercise more choice in becoming gay than they believe or are willing to say. I came away thinking that for many, that probably is so. But it is also clear that some features of some people's sexualities are determined by factors beyond their control, making "amenability to conscious choice" one of the many individually variable dimensions of human sexualities.[2] And some individuals might well be born with characteristics that— *in particular cultural contexts*—will point them toward becoming gay.[3] The problem is that "Is it a choice?" is an uninteresting yes-or-no question. I have used the idea of choice not to answer it, but to drive a wedge into understanding what sexual preference is.

The concept of sexual preference creates a binary distinction between the heterosexual and the homosexual. This research calls that binary construction into question. Relying on that dichotomy, most lesbians and gay men present their life stories so as to maximize consistency and continuity.[4] Those who do not, for whatever reason, rely on that dichotomy—notably, the bisexuals and the lesbian-feminists—invoke the concept of choice. Claiming choice is, consciously or not, a way to refuse to place oneself into the homosexual/heterosexual binary. It is the wedge that disrupts one of the most powerful concepts structuring sexuality in the modern West.

We need to distinguish the theoretical usefulness of the concept of choice from the definitive description of how sexual preference is experienced. As respondents repeatedly stated, the notion that one chooses to be gay overrationalizes sex, describing it in language that has been commandeered by the culture of consumer capitalism. They're right: We don't choose our sexualities the way we choose a breakfast cereal. We most fondly hope that our sexuality taps into emotions, desires, and fears that run deeper than that. But we often construct ideas to fulfill this hope that are rigid and reifying. Our sexual desires can only be summed up neatly as either heterosexual or homosexual if we ignore the vast variations within those categories and the change and uncertainly in individual experience. Individual sexualities may not be endlessly changeable, but they are more changeable than most of us think. Even if there are essential differences among individuals, there is no reason to assume that current categories accurately capture them.

This book has been concerned with questioning dichotomies, but it has also questioned unities. I have tried to demonstrate, in particular, how the dominant account serves to construct unity, to create sameness and conceal difference. The concept of homosexuality itself (and, certainly, heterosexuality also) does the same. Underneath, there is probably another conceptual false unity of desire itself. The common pairings—heterosexual/homosexual, lesbian/gay, conceived as matched opposites—imply that sexual desire takes one form, and that only its object varies. By this formula, we merely insert new details into an overall structure of desire that is always the same. By emphasizing variation, I would hope to have shaken such a unity of desire. The individuals who have spoken in these pages don't necessarily all share the same orientation, even though they do share the same preference.

The political dangers of a choice discourse go beyond the simple (if controversial) notion that some people genuinely choose their homosexuality. Indeed, my conclusions question some of the fundamental bases upon which the gay- and lesbian-rights movement has been built. If we cannot make political claims based on an essential and shared nature, are we not left once again as individual deviants? Without an essentialist foundation, do we have a viable politics?

These questions are being asked by many individuals and organizations in a variety of settings, not all of them lesbian/gay. The answers will be hammered out through the interplay of scholarly production and political action; the definitive solution won't be found here. I do believe that the critique of identity politics will open up valuable new possibilities for political intervention even as it questions some old ones. Nonetheless, the dilemma is real. In a review of Flax (1990), hooks (1990), and Butler (1990), Bordo sums it up nicely:

> While rightly eschewing essentialist notions of race and gender, both [Flax and hooks] are nonetheless suspicious of any fragmentation which would undermine the authority of our experience just at that cultural moment when we might begin to "remember ourselves" and "to make ourselves subject." (1992: 163)

The dilemma expresses the crucial divide in lesbian and gay politics at present. On the one hand is a minority-model approach that seeks equality and civil remedies for a (presumably clearly defined) homosexual minority in a world dominated by a heterosexual majority. This approach represents exactly what a good number of gay men—and lesbians—want: the ability to go about their lives without being variously encumbered, to say nothing of endangered, by a range of negative social responses to their sexual preferences. They neither have nor see the need for a radical and critical analysis of the underlying structure of the society that oppresses them. On the other hand are a number of so far only loosely connected approaches that are highly critical of the underlying structures of sexuality, gender, and family that characterize contemporary Western societies. This approach includes, though is not necessarily defined by, a critique of the heterosexual-homosexual binary that the minoritizing approach rests upon. Being gay is at one and the same time like being left-handed, as Randy Shilts put it, and much, much more. Sedgwick (1990) calls these approaches minoritizing and universalizing, respectively, while Snitow (1990) names the parallel tendencies in feminist activism maximizing and minimizing. Both recommend that the tension between them be used rather than resolved, that, in Sedgwick's words, we "underwrite continuously the legitimacy of both" approaches.

But just what that might mean is difficult to see when those two approaches suggest strategies that are quite opposed to one another. In any particular legal case, for example, the simultaneous use of both would likely appear disorganized and contradictory. So while it we may enjoy the creative chaos of a movement that cannot be pinned down to a consistent position, we do still need to envision forms of discourse that are not limited to one of these two poles. To that end, it seems to me that identity politics is at its richest in those areas where groups of individuals share more than one stigmatized identity. Those who are both women and gay are precisely those whose group, or minority, interests push for a more radical analysis.

Steven Seidman (1993, 1994) argues similarly that the mobilization of lesbian and gay people of color in the 1980s provided the social context for the development of queer theory. Those whose queer identities are not predicated on gender, racial/ethnic, and other forms of dominance are best positioned to comprehend "the gain of figuring identity as permanently open as to its meaning and political use" (1994: 173). As such, a queer movement that featured the empowered participation of lesbians and gay men of color, white lesbians, and bisexuals would give rise to forms of action and analysis that could resolve some of the tensions between minoritizing and universalizing tendencies, between poles that are oversimply referred to as "essentialist politics" and "constructionist theory."

We must also begin to recognize and utilize the very political uniqueness of sexual preference instead of relying on facile parallels with race and gender. Since queerness visibly marks an individual only imperfectly and sporadically, prejudice, discrimination, harassment, and violence are heaped upon those who are *perceived* to be homosexual. That perception is based on gender performance as much as actual information about how and with whom one loves, builds relationships, and has sex. While legal remedies that seek to protect the civil rights of lesbians, gay men, and bisexuals generally recognize the possibility of mistaken identity, other approaches might begin with this point.

To my mind, the most promising arena is the broad area of "family politics." This loose cluster of movements and issues concerns relationships among people—which ones are recognized and privileged and which ones are not. As Weston (1990) has shown, with whom we have sex is only one piece of our lives as lesbians and gay men. If and how one parents, with whom one shares economic resources, housing, and a personal history, to whom one turns for help and support: these features of gay and lesbian lives are more material than the issues of selfhood and identity captured by the minority-rights approach. The politics built on these does not always depend on types of persons, and in fact cuts across those handily, providing opportunities for coalitions among a variety of groups who share an interest in changing family structure.

Broadly defined, "family" may be the name we can use to refer to the experience, as opposed to the essence, that we share. hooks makes a point about black essence and experience that parallels the distinction we need to make in lesbian and gay politics.

> There is a radical difference between a repudiation of the idea that there is a black "essence" and recognition of the way black identity has been specifically constituted in the experience of exile and struggle. (1990: 29)

Part of this shared experience has been captured in the concept of "queerness": a recognition that living as sexual outlaws is what unites us, not a shared and essential identity. But by beginning with the isolated individual, queerness is biased toward male experience.[5] Family politics, in its emphasis on relationships—including but certainly not limited to erotic and romantic pairs—begins with the reality of social connection.

Finally, what does this study imply for the future of lesbian-feminism? While I have emphasized the critique of the mainstream gay-rights movement, it is lesbian-feminism that is receiving the most public criticism at this point. In what is partly a battle fought out between generation-X and baby-boomer women, and partly the lingering effects of the "sex wars," the lesbian-feminist movement has been the target of often vicious criticism (see Stein 1992, 1993; Whisman 1994).

Despite the very real problems manifest in some of the tenets and practices of lesbian-feminism, its offhand dismissal by scholars and activists is foolish. Lesbian-feminist theory still provides much that is lacking in gay theory and politics, particularly its critique of the heterosexual-homosexual binary and its recognition of the relationship between the subordination of all women and the oppression of gay men and lesbians. Although it tends toward essentialist gender conceptions—stereotypical notions of male and female natures—lesbian-feminism's understanding of sexuality has always been constructionist.

The currently popular portrayal of constructionist and lesbian-feminist theories as opposed to one another is misleading. My analysis has relied on both. Therefore, a further political implication of this work is the suggestion that new forms of lesbian organizing must take into account what is valuable in lesbian-feminism. As Creet points out:

> Since at least the late '60s, lesbians have been linked by one set of needs and analysis or another with both the feminist and gay movements. We will always have to negotiate between the two (at least). (1991:32)

If lesbians are to survive—and more, if we are to use the wisdom of our particular experience to push for ways of social organizing that will liberate others as well as ourselves—we cannot let our political agenda be swallowed either by the male gay movement or the heterosexual feminist movement.

What, finally, of accounts? My analysis suggests that we allow them to proliferate. If homosexuality is a point around which we cluster, let the paths for reaching that point be visible. One person arrives there because of a deeply felt physical desire for others of the same sex, another for a desire that is more emotional than physical. One woman arrives there because she has chosen to explore feelings for women and extinguish those for men, because her feminist understanding tells her that is the best choice for her. Another woman has felt different all her life, more masculine than feminine. One man has always been sexually interested in both men and women, and finds queer worlds more to his liking than straight ones. There is no essential Gay Man, no timeless Lesbian, but instead gay men, lesbians, bisexuals, and others, who collectively and individually widen the range of possibilities.

Notes

1. A few of the lesbian-feminists, although they understood their lesbianism as chosen, believed that their feminism somehow natural to them. In that, they follow the pattern in lesbian-feminist theory whereby sexual preference is understood as socially constructed while gender differences are portrayed as essential.

2. For beginning lists of some of these undertheorized dimensions, see Bem (1993), Newton and Walton (1984) and Sedgwick (1990).

3. Even the most cursory examination of cultural and historical variation suggests that it is preposterous to imagine that what we in the modern West now conceptualize as homosexuality is innate (see Newton 1988).

4. People who identify themselves as heterosexual are also generally inclined to downplay or explain away their homosexual behavior. At its most extreme, this desire can create a reaction-formation of extreme homophobia. See Blumstein and Schwartz 1976a, 1976b, 1977; Herek 1985.

5. Queer Nation, the now almost entirely disbanded organization that most utilized the queer politics approach, was frequently called on its androcentric assumptions. See Gray 1992; Maggenti 1993.

Appendix

Methodology

The individuals interviewed constitute a volunteer sample. Although they came to the study through a variety of recruitment sources (see Tables A.1 and A.2), every respondent initially contacted me. That procedure, although unavoidable, does bias the sample toward outgoing, socially involved respondents. As Table A.3 indicates, gay men and lesbians who are very highly involved in lesbian and gay community life are certainly over-represented.

Table A.1: Recruitment, Lesbians

Source	Number of respondents	
Advertisements in publications		20 (51%)
lesbian/feminist publications	12 (31%)	
general audience publications	8 (21%)	
Flyers		7 (18%)
bars	3 (8%)	
Gay and Lesbian Community Center	3 (8%)	
other	1 (3%)	
Organizational contacts		4 (10%)
gay/lesbian organizations	2 (5%)	
lesbian/feminist organizations	2 (5%)	
Snowball		8 (21%)
TOTAL		39 (100%)[1]

[1] In this and following tables, totals may not add to exactly 100%, due to rounding error.

Table A.2: Recruitment, Gay Men

Source	Number of respondents	
Advertisements in publications		15 (45%)
gay publications	9 (27%)	
general audience publications	6 (18%)	
Flyers		12 (36%)
bars	7 (21%)	
Lesbian and Gay Community Center	3 (9%)	
other	2 (6%)	
Organizational contacts		3 (9%)
gay/lesbian organizations	2 (6%)	
gay men's organizations	1 (3%)	
Snowball		3 (9%)
TOTAL		33 (100%)

Table A.3: Respondents' Levels of Gay/Lesbian Community Involvement[2]

Level of involvement	Gay Men	Lesbians	TOTAL
private	7 (21%)	11 (28%)	17 (24%)
public	15 (45%)	19 (49%)	35 (49%)
very high	11 (33%)	9 (23%)	20 (28%)
TOTAL	33(100%)	39(100%)	72(100%)

[2] Definitions: An individual whose involvement is defined as "private" has lesbian or gay friends, and/or reads lesbian/gay publications, but does not attend meetings, events, the bars, or other gatherings in public space. One respondent is included in this group whose only contact with other gay men/lesbians is a therapy group.

An individual whose involvement is defined as "public" is involved in gay and lesbian activities that take place in public space. Some frequent the bars; others attend meetings, benefits, gay and lesbian 12-step groups, or demonstrations, and others are members of formal organizations, which may be social or political in purpose.

An individual was defined as "very involved" if her or his life included all the forms of involvement noted in the previous definitions. Of these most active respondents, 7 men and 3 women would be considered leaders, in the sense that they actually have founded, or hold office in, a formal organization.

Most recruitment contacts were general, seeking gay men and/or lesbians to participate in a study, and some targeted specific populations. Efforts to diversify the sample sought people of color or people over the age of forty. Some contacts were also aimed at finding respondents of the "chosen"-account group, particularly men. This oversampling of otherwise under-represented populations seems appropriate in research which makes no quantitative predictions about the distribution of variables in the total population.

Despite some targeted sampling, the respondents as a group are younger, more educated and more middle-class than the gay and lesbian population. However, the comparative technique used—comparisons of percentages across categories of the dependent variable within a given category of the independent variable—is not biased by the unrepresentative nature of the sample. Additionally, by oversampling in one category of the dependent variable I have lessened a real difference in the population and biased my tables toward lesser magnitude of between-group differences. Barring the collection of an enormous sample, however—which usually prohibits the use of in-depth interviewing—"chosen"-account respondents must be oversampled in order to identify any at all, particular among men.

I interviewed seventy-seven people, five of whom do not appear in the sample. Two of those were male-to-female transsexuals, whose interviews will appear in subsequent reports. The other unused interviews wandered significantly from the subject matter and/or were internally inconsistent.

I chose the final sample size of 72 for convenience. Eventually, additional interviewing in the "mixed"-account category ceased to provide any new information; nonetheless, most contacts offered that account. Even calls for people who had chosen to be gay located more "mixed"- than "chosen"- account respondents, as I discuss in Chapter Three. Pre-interview screening on such a complex matter was impossible; final placement in one of the typology categories was based on material from throughout the interview as no one question truly captured it. And so I finally stopped interviewing new respondents, even though I would have liked to find more "chosen"-account men.

Sample Characteristics

Table A.4: Account Type			
	Gay men	**Lesbians**	**TOTAL**
Determined	5 (15%)	4 (10%)	9 (12%)
Mixed	22 (67%)	23 (59%)	45 (62%)
Chosen	6 (18%)	12 (31%)	18 (25%)
TOTAL	33 (100%)	39 (100%)	72(100%)

Table A.5: Age

	Gay Men		Lesbians		TOTAL	
16 – 20	0	(0%)	1	(3%)	1	(1%)
21 – 25	4	(12%)	13	(33%)	17	(24%)
26 – 30	9	(27%)	9	(23%)	18	(25%)
31 – 35	9	(27%)	10	(26%)	19	(26%)
36 – 40	2	(6%)	3	(8%)	5	(7%)
41 – 45	3	(9%)	2	(5%)	5	(7%)
46 – 50	2	(6%)	0	(0%)	2	(3%)
51 – 55	2	(6%)	0	(0%)	2	(3%)
56 – 60	1	(3%)	1	(3%)	1	(1%)
61 +	1	(3%)	0	(0%)	1	(1%)
TOTAL	33	(100%)	39	(100%)	72	(100%)

Table A.6: Race/ethnicity[3]

	Gay Men		Lesbians		TOTAL	
People of color	6	(18%)	9	(23%)	15	(21%)
White anglo	27	(82%)	30	(77%)	57	(79%)
TOTAL	33	(100%)	39	(100%)	72	(100%)

[3] Latina/os are counted here as people of color, whatever their racial background.

Table A.7: Place of Origin

	Gay Men		Lesbians		TOTAL	
New York City metro area	11	(33%)	20	(51%)	31	(43%)
Outside NYC:						
urban	10	(30%)	12	(31%)	22	(31%)
small cities	10	(30%)	7	(18%)	17	(24%)
rural	2	(6%)	0	(0%)	2	(3%)
TOTAL	33	(100%)	39	(100%)	72	(100%)

Table A.8: Annual Income

	Gay Men		Lesbians		TOTAL	
$ 0 – 4,999	1	(3%)	2	(5%)	3	(4%)
5,000 – 9,999	1	(3%)	4	(10%)	5	(7%)
10,000 – 14,999	2	(6%)	7	(18%)	9	(12%)
15,000 – 19,999	9	(27%)	6	(15%)	15	(21%)
20,000 – 24,999	4	(12%)	9	(23%)	13	(18%)
25,000 – 29,999	4	(12%)	8	(21%)	12	(17%)
30,000 – 34,999	1	(3%)	0	(0%)	1	(1%)
35,000 – 44,999	6	(18%)	0	(0%)	6	(8%)
45,000 – 59,999	0	(0%)	0	(0%)	0	(0%)
60,000 – 79,999	1	(3%)	0	(0%)	1	(1%)
80,000 +	2	(6%)	0	(0%)	2	(3%)
missing	2	(6%)		3(8%)	5	(7%)
TOTAL	33	(100%)	39	(100%)	72	(100%)

Table A.9: Education

	Gay Men		Lesbians		TOTAL	
Some graduate education	8	(24%)	9	(23%)	17	(24%)
4 – year degree	12	(36%)	11	(28%)	23	(32%)
2 – 4 yrs college	9	(27%)	9	(23%)	18	(25%)
< 2 yrs college	3	(9%)	4	(10%)	7	(10%)
H.S. or GED	1	(3%)	5	(13%)	6	(8%)
Missing	0	(0%)	1	(3%)	1	(1%)
TOTAL	33	(100%)	39	(100%)	72	(100%)

Table A.10: Religion[4]

	Gay Men		Lesbians		TOTAL	
Catholic	13	(39%)	16	(41%)	29	(40%)
Jewish	5	(15%)	7	(18%)	12	(17%)
Protestant	13	(39%)	13	(33%)	26	(36%)
none	2	(6%)	3	(8%)	5	(7%)
TOTAL	33	(100%)	39	(100%)	72	(100%)

[4] Refers to the religious tradition in which the respondent was raised, not her/his current affiliation.

Findings

The tables which follow provide data for findings discussed in the text, particularly in Chapter Four. I used a Chi-square test for significance only as a criterion for determining which relationships were of sufficient magnitude to discuss in my analysis. I provide those values here for the reader's information, and not to suggest that these findings are predictive for any larger population.

Table A.11: Account Type by Continuous Awareness of Sexual Orientation[5]

LESBIANS	Continuity		Discontinuity		TOTAL	
Determined	4	(36%)	0	(0%)	4	(10%)
Mixed	6	(55%)	17	(61%)	23	(59%)
Chosen	1	(9%)	11	(39%)	12	(31%)
TOTAL	11	(100%)	28	(100%)	39	(100%)

GAY MEN	Continuity		Discontinuity		TOTAL	
Determined	4	(20%)	1	(8%)	5	(15%)
Mixed	15	(75%)	7	(54%)	22	(67%)
Chosen	1	(5%)	5	(38%)	6	(18%)
TOTAL	20	(100%)	13	(100%)	33	(100%)

[5] Lesbians: Chi-square 12.55, dof = 2, p <.01
Gay Men: Chi-square 6.18, dof = 2, p <.05

Table A.12: Account Type by Childhood Gender Presentation[6]

LESBIANS	Feminine		Tomboy		TOTAL	
Determined	1	(5%)	3	(15%)	4	(10%)
Mixed	10	(53%)	13	(65%)	23	(59%)
Chosen	8	(42%)	4	(20%)	12	(31%)
TOTAL	20	(100%)	19	(100%)	39	(100%)

GAY MEN	Masculine		Effeminate		TOTAL	
Determined	1	(6%)	4	(24%)	5	(15%)
Mixed	10	(62%)	12	(71%)	22	(67%)
Chosen	5	(31%)	1	(6%)	6	(18%)
TOTAL	16	(100%)	17	(100%)	33	(100%)

[6] Lesbians: Chi-square 2.69, dof = 2, not significant
Gay Men: Chi-square 4.60, dof = 2, p < .10

Table A.13: Account Type by Heterosexual Sexual Experience[7]

LESBIANS	No Experience		Some Experience		TOTAL	
Determined	2	(19%)	2	(6%)	4	(10%)
Mixed	3	(43%)	20	(62%)	23	(59%)
Chosen	2	(29%)	10	(31%)	12	(31%)
TOTAL	7	(100%)	32	(100%)	39	(100%)

GAY MEN	No Experience		Some Experience		TOTAL	
Determined	3	(25%)	2	(10%)	5	(15%)
Mixed	9	(75%)	13	(62%)	22	(67%)
Chosen	0	(0%)	6	(29%)	6	(18%)
TOTAL	12	(100%)	21	(100%)	33	(100%)

[7]   Lesbians: Chi-square 3.16, dof = 2, not significant
Gay Men: Chi-square 4.82, dof = 2, $p < .10$

Table A.14: Account Type by Involvement in Meaningful Heterosexual Relationship(s)[8]

LESBIANS	No Involvement		Some Involvement		TOTAL	
Determined	4	(36%)	0	(0%)	4	(10%)
Mixed	6	(55%)	17	(61%)	23	(59%)
Chosen	1	(9%)	11	(39%)	12	(31%)
TOTAL	11	(100%)	28	(100%)	39	(100%)

GAY MEN	No Involvement		Some Involvement		TOTAL	
Determined	4	(22%)	1	(7%)	5	(15%)
Mixed	12	(67%)	10	(67%)	22	(67%)
Chosen	2	(11%)	4	(27%)	6	(18%)
TOTAL	18	(100%)	15	(100%)	33	(100%)

[8]   Lesbians: Chi-square 12.53, dof = 2, $p < .01$
Gay Men: Chi-square 2.38, dof = 2, not significant

Table A.15: Account Type by Bisexual Identification[9]

LESBIANS	Not Bisexual		Somewhat Bisexual		TOTAL	
Determined	3	(12%)	1	(8%)	4	(10%)
Mixed	19	(73%)	4	(31%)	23	(59%)
Chosen	4	(15%)	8	(62%)	12	(31%)
TOTAL	26	(100%)	13	(100%)	39	(100%)

GAY MEN	Not Bisexual		Somewhat Bisexual		TOTAL	
Determined	5	(20%)	0	(0%)	5	(15%)
Mixed	17	(68%)	5	(62%)	22	(67%)
Chosen	3	(12%)	3	(38%)	6	(18%)
TOTAL	25	(100%)	8	(100%)	33	(100%)

[9] Lesbians: Chi-square 8.76, dof = 2, $p < .05$
Gay Men: Chi-square 3.82, dof = 2, not significant

Table A.16: Account Type by Coming-Out Cohort[10]

LESBIANS	Before 1970		1970s		1980s		TOTAL	
Determined	0	(0%)	3	(27%)	1	(4%)	4	(10%)
Mixed	4	(80%)	4	(36%)	15	(65%)	23	(59%)
Chosen	1	(20%)	4	(36%)	7	(30%)	12	(31%)
TOTAL	5	(100%)	11	(100%)	23	(100%)	39	(100%)

GAY MEN	Before 1969		After 1969		TOTAL	
Determined	4	(50%)	1	(4%)	5	(15%)
Mixed	3	(38%)	19	(76%)	22	(67%)
Chosen	1	(12%)	5	(20%)	6	(18%)
TOTAL	8	(100%)	25	(100%)	33	(100%)

[10] Lesbians: Not significant. However, when categories representing those who came out prior to 1970 and those who came out after 1979 are collapsed, the relationship between account type and decade of coming out (1970s vs. all others) is significant. Chi-square 5.82, dof = 2, $p < .10$
Gay Men: Chi-square 10.37, dof = 2, $p < .01$

Table A.17: Account Type by Race[11]

LESBIANS	White/anglo		Women of Color		TOTAL	
Determined	4	(12%)	0	(0%)	4	(10%)
Mixed	18	(60%)	5	(56%)	23	(59%)
Chosen	8	(27%)	4	(44%)	12	(31%)
TOTAL	30	(100%)	9	(100%)	39	(100%)

GAY MEN	White/anglo		Men of Color		TOTAL	
Determined	4	(15%)	1	(17%)	5	(15%)
Mixed	17	(63%)	5	(83%)	22	(67%)
Chosen	6	(22%)	0	(0%)	6	(18%)
TOTAL	27	(100%)	6	(100%)	33	(100%)

[11]   Lesbians: Chi-square 1.94, dof = 2, not significant
Gay Men: Chi-square 1.65, dof = 2, not significant

Table A.18: Account Type by Religious Background[12]

LESBIANS	Catholic		Jewish		Protestant		None		TOTAL	
Determined	1	(6%)	1	(14%)	2	(15%)	0	(0%)	4	(10%)
Mixed	12	(75%)	4	(57%)	6	(46%)	1	(33%)	23	(59%)
Chosen	3	(19%)	2	(29%)	5	(38%)	2	(67%)	12	(31%)
TOTAL	16	(100%)	7	(100%)	13	(100%)	3	(100%)	39	(100%)

GAY MEN	Catholic		Jewish		Protestant		None		TOTAL	
Determined	0	(0%)	1	(20%)	3	(20%)	1	(50%)	5	(15%)
Mixed	8	(73%)	3	(60%)	10	(67%)	1	(50%)	22	(67%)
Chosen	3	(27%)	1	(20%)	2	(13%)	0	(0%)	6	(18%)
TOTAL	11	(100%)	5	(100%)	15	(100%)	2	(100%)	33	(100%)

[12]   Lesbians: Chi-square 5.90, dof = 6, not significant
Gay men: Chi-square 5.37, dof = 6, not significant

Table A.19: Account Type by Annual Income[13]

LESBIANS	$0–9,999		$10–19,999		$20,000+		TOTAL	
Determined	1	(20%)	1	(8%)	1	(6%)	3	(8%)
Mixed	3	(60%)	8	(62%)	12	(67%)	23	(64%)
Chosen	1	(20%)	4	(31%)	5	(28%)	10	(28%)
TOTAL	5	(100%)	13	(100%)	18	(100%)	36	(100%)

GAY MEN	$0 –9,999		$10,000 –19,999		$20,000 –29,999		$30,000		TOTAL	
Determined	0	(0%)	1	(9%)	1	(12%)	3	(30%)	5	(16%)
Mixed	2	(100%)	8	(73%)	6	(75%)	5	(50%)	21	(68%)
Chosen	0	(0%)	2	(18%)	1	(12%)	2	(20%)	5	(16%)
TOTAL	2	(100%)	11	(100%)	8	(100%)	10	(100%)	31	(100%)

[13] Lesbians: N = 36, with three missing cases. Chi-square 1.12, dof = 4, not significant

Gay Men: N = 31, with two missing cases. Chi-square 4.22, dof = 6, not significant

Table A.20: Account type by occupation[14]

LESBIANS	Level I		Level II		TOTAL	
Determined	2	(12%)	2	(15%)	4	(14%)
Mixed	8	(50%)	8	(62%)	16	(55%)
Chosen	6	(38%)	3	(23%)	9	(31%)
TOTAL	16	(100%)	13	(100%)	29	(100%)

GAY MEN	Level I		Level II		TOTAL	
Determined	0	(0%)	5	(18%)	5	(15%)
Mixed	10	(40%)	10	(56%)	20	(71%)
Chosen	0	(0%)	3	(17%)	3	(11%)
TOTAL	10	(100%)	18	(100%)	28	(100%)

[14] Full-time students are not included here. Occupational Level I includes clerical workers, service workers, and blue-collar workers (including women in traditionally male-dominated trades). Level II includes managers, technical workers, and professionals (the majority teachers and social workers).
Lesbians: Chi-square 1.58, dof = 2, not significant
Gay Men: Chi-square 6.24, dof = 2, p < .05

Table A.21: Average Ages at Coming Out[15]

	Women	Men	Total
Mean	20	18	19
Median	20	19	19
Range	12–3	15–30	5–31

[15] For the difference of means between lesbians and gay men, t = 1.69, p < .05. (One-tailed test used to ascertain whether or not gay men come out earlier than lesbians.)

Bibliography

Adam, Barry. 1987. *The Rise of a Gay and Lesbian Movement*. Boston:Twayne.

Alderfer, Hannah et al., 1982. *Diary of a Conference on Sexuality*. New York: Barnard Women's Center.

Almaguer, Tomás. 1990. "The cartography of homosexual desire and identity among Chicano men." Paper presented at the Lesbian, Gay and Bisexual Studies Conference, Harvard University, October 26–28.

Altman, Dennis. 1982. *The Homosexualization of America*. Boston: Beacon.

Anzaldua, Gloria, ed. 1990. *Making Face, Making Soul*. San Francisco: Aunt Lute Foundation.

Badgett, Lee. 1994. "Economic evidence of sexual-orientation discrmination." Paper presented at The Center for Lesbian and Gay Studies, Graduate Center of the City University of New York, May 7.

Bell, Alan P. and Martin S. Weinberg. 1978. *Homosexualities*. New York: Simon and Schuster.

Bell, Alan, Martin Weinberg and Sue Hammersmith. 1981. *Sexual Preference: Its Development in Men and Women*. Bloomington: Indiana University Press.

Bem, Sandra Lipsitz. 1993. *The Lenses of Gender: Transforming the Debate on Sexual Inequality*. New Haven: Yale University Press.

Blumenfeld, Warren, ed. 1992. *Homophobia: How We All Pay the Price*. Boston: Beacon Press.

Blumstein, Philip and Pepper Schwartz. 1976a. "Bisexuality in men." *Urban Life* 5:79–98.

———. 1976b. "Bisexuality in women." *Archives of Sexual Behavior* 5:171–81.

————. 1977. "Bisexuality: Some social psychological issues." *Journal of Social Issues* 33:30–45.

————. 1979. "The acquisition of sexual identity." Revised version of a paper presented at the annual meetings of the American Sociological Association, Montreal, August 1974.

————. 1983. *American Couples.* New York: William Morrow.

Bordo, Susan. 1992. "Postmodern subjects, postmodern bodies." *Feminist Studies* 18:159–175.

Bunch, Charlotte. 1984. "Lesbians in revolt." In *Feminist Frameworks: Alternative Theoretical Accounts of the Relations Between Women and Men,* 2nd ed., edited by Alison Jaggar and Paula Rothenberg. New York: McGraw-Hill.

Butler, Judith. 1990. *Gender Trouble: Feminism and the Subversion of Identity.* New York: Routledge.

Card, Claudia. 1995. *Lesbian Choices.* New York: Columbia University Press.

Carrigan, Tim, Bob Connell and John Lee. 1985. "Toward a new sociology of masculinity." *Theory and Society* 14:551–604.

Carr, C. 1992. "Reclaiming our *Basic* rights." *Village Voice* April 28:35–36.

Cass, Vivienne. 1979. "Homosexual identity formation: A theoretical model." *Journal of Homosexuality* 4:219–35.

Chauncey, George. 1982–83. "From sexual inversion to homosexuality: Medicine and the changing conceptualization of female deviance." *Salmagundi* 58–59 (Fall–Winter):114–46.

Clausen, Jan. 1990. "My interesting condition." *Out/Look* 7:10–21.

Collins, Randall. 1974. *Conflict Sociology: Toward an Explanatory Science.* New York: Academic Press.

Combahee River Collective. 1979. "A Black feminist statement." In Z. Eisenstein, ed., *Capitalist Patriarchy and the Case for Socialist Feminism.* New York: Monthly Review.

Connell, R.W. 1987. *Gender and Power.* Stanford: Stanford University Press.

Cooper, Dennis. 1992. "Johnny Noxzema to the gay community: 'You are the enemy.'" *Village Voice* 37(26):31–33.

Corradi, Consuelo. 1991. "Text, context and individual meaning: Rethinking life stories in a hermeneutic framework." *Discourse and Society* 2:105–18.

Creet, Julia. 1991. "Lesbian sex/gay sex: What's the difference?" *Out/Look* 11:29–34.

D'Adesky, Anne-Christine. 1994. "Brave new gene." *Out* July/August:108–16.

Dank, Barry. 1979. "Coming out in the gay world." In *Gay Men: The Sociology of Male Homosexuality,* edited by Martin Levine. New York: Harper Colophon.

D'Emilio, John. 1983a. *Sexual Politics, Sexual Communities.* Chicago: University of Chicago.

————. 1983b. "Capitalism and gay identity." In *Powers of Desire,* edited by Ann Snitow, et al. New York: Monthly Review.

————. 1992. *Making Trouble: Essays on Gay History, Politics, and the University.* New York: Routledge.

de Beauvoir, Simone. 1952. *The Second Sex.* New York: Alfred A. Knopf, Inc.

DeMonteflores, Carmen and Stephen Schultz. 1978. "Coming out: Similarities and differences for lesbians and gay men." *Journal of Social Issues* 34:59–72.

DeWitt, Karen. 1992. "Quayle contends homosexuality is a matter of choice, not biology." *New York Times*, September 14:A17.

Ehrenreich, Barbara. 1979. *For Her Own Good: 150 Years of the Experts' Advice to Women*. Garden City: Anchor Press.

Elliot, Stuart. 1994. "A sharper view of gay consumers." *New York Times*, June 9:D1,19.

Ellis, Havelock. 1928. "Sexual inversion." In *Studies in the Psychology of Sex*. Philadelphia: F.A. Davis.

Epstein, Steven. 1987. "Gay politics, ethnic identity: The limits of social constructionism." *Socialist Review* 17:9–54.

——— . 1988. "Nature vs. Nurture and the politics of AIDS organizing." *Out/Look* 3:46–53.

Ernulf, Kurt, Sune Innala and Frederick Whitam. 1989. "Biological explanation, psychological explanation, and tolerance of homosexuals: A cross-national analysis of beliefs and attitudes." *Psychological Reports* 65:1003–1010.

Ettore, E.M. 1980. *Lesbians, Women, and Society*. London: Routledge and Kegan Paul.

Faderman, Lillian. 1981. *Surpassing the Love of Men*. New York: William Morrow.

——— . 1991. *Odd Girls and Twilight Lovers*. New York: Columbia University.

Faraday, Annabel. 1981. "Liberating lesbian research." In *The Making of the Modern Homosexual*, edited by Kenneth Plummer. London: Hutchinson.

Ferguson, Ann. 1981. "Patriarchy, sexual identity, and the sexual revolution." *Signs* 7:158–72.

——— et al. 1984. "Forum: The feminist sexuality debates." *Signs* 10: 106–35.

Fernandez, Charles. 1991. "Undocumented aliens in the queer nation." *Out/Look* 3(3):20–23.

Firestone, Shulamith. 1970. *The Dialectic of Sex: The Case for Feminist Revolution*. New York: Willian Morrow and Company.

Flax, Jane. 1990. *Thinking Fragments: Psychoanalysis, Feminism, and Postmodernism in the Contemporary West*. Berkeley: University of California. Freud, Sigmund. 1962. "The sexual aberrations." In *Three Essays on the Theory of Sexuality*. New York: Basic.

Fuss, Diana. 1989. *Essentially Speaking: Feminism, Nature and Difference*. New York: Routledge.

Gagnon, John. 1977. *Human Sexualities*. Glenview, Ill: Scott, Foresman.

——— and William Simon. 1973. *Sexual Conduct*. Chicago: Aldine.

Gallagher, Bob and Alexander Wilson. 1987. "Sex and the politics of identity: An interview with Michel Foucault." In *Gay Spirit: Myth and Meaning*, edited by Mark Thompson. New York: St. Martin's Press.

Gelman, David, et al. 1992. "Born or bred?" *Newsweek*, February 24:46–53.

Gessen, Masha. 1989. "Fishing for our rights." *Next* 2(9):10–11.

Gilligan, Carol. 1982. *In a Different Voice: Psychological Theory and Women's Development*. Cambridge, Mass.: Harvard.

Ginsburg, Faye. 1984. "The body politic: The defense of sexual restriction by anti-abortion activists." In *Pleasure and Danger*, edited by Carole Vance. Boston: Routledge and Kegan Paul.

Golden, Carla. 1987. "Diversity and variability in women's sexual identities." In *Lesbian Psychologies*, edited by The Boston Lesbian Psychologies Collective. Urbana: University of Illinois.

Goss, Robert. 1993. *Jesus Acted Up: A Gay and Lesbian Manifesto*. San Francisco: Harper Collins.

Gramick, Jeanine. 1984. "Developing a lesbian identity." In *Women-Identified Women*, edited by Trudy Darty and Sandee Potter. Palo Alto, Calif.: Mayfield.

Gray, Natasha. 1992. "Bored with the boys: Cracks in the queer coalition." *NYQ*, April 26:26–30.

Green, Richard. 1987. *The "Sissy Boy Syndrome"*. New Haven: Yale University Press.

———. 1993. "On homosexual orientation as an immutable characteristic." In *Gays and the Military*, edited by Marc Wolinsky and Kenneth Sherrill. Princeton: Princeton University.

Greenberg, David. 1988. *The Construction of Homosexuality*. Chicago: University of Chicago.

Hall, Radclyffe. 1928. *The Well of Loneliness*. London: Jonathan Cape.

Hall Carpenter Archives. 1989. *Inventing Ourselves: Lesbian Life Stories*. London: Routledge.

Halley, Janet. 1993. "Reasoning about sodomy: Act and identity in and after *Bowers v. Hardwick*." *Virginia Law Review* 79:1721–80.

Halperin, David. 1994. "The queer politics of Michel Foucault." Paper presented at Cornell University Society for the Humanities, February 18.

Hamer, Dean, Stella Hu, Victoria Magnuson, Nan Hu, and Angela Pattatucci. 1993. "A linkage between DNA markers on the X chromosome and male sexual orientation." *Science* 261:321–27.

Harry, Joseph. 1984. "Sexual orientation as destiny." *Journal of Homosexuality* 10:111–24.

Hart, John. 1984. "Therapeutic implications of viewing sexual identity in terms of essentialist and constructionist theories." *Journal of Homosexuality* 9:39–52.

Hawkeswood, William. 1991. *"One of the Children": An Ethnography of Identity and Gay Black Men*. Unpublished dissertation, Department of Anthropology, Columbia University.

Herek, Gregory. 1985. "Beyond 'homophobia.'" In *Bashers, Baiters and Bigots*, edited by John DeCecco. New York: Harrington Park Press.

———. 1987. "On heterosexual masculinity: Some psychical consequences of the social constsruction of gender and sexuality." In *Changing Men*, edited by Michael Kimmel. Newbury Park, Calif.: Sage Publications.

Hollibaugh, Amber and Cherrie Moraga. 1981. "What we're rollin' around in bed with." *Heresies: A Feminist Publication on Art and Politics* 3(4):58–62.

Holmes, Sarah, ed. 1988. *Testimonies: A Collection of Lesbian Coming Out Stories*. Boston: Alyson Publications.

hooks, bell. 1990. *Yearning: Race, Gender, and Cultural Politics*. Boston: South End Press.

——— and Cornel West. 1991. *Breaking Bread: Insurgent Black Intellectual Life*. Boston: South End.

Humphreys, Laud. 1970. *Tearoom Trade: Impersonal Sex in Public Places*. Chicago: Aldine.

Hutchins, Loraine and Lani Kaahumanu. 1991. *Bi Any Other Name: Bisexual People Speak Out*. Boston: Alyson Publications.

Johnston, Jill. 1973. *Lesbian Nation: The Feminist Solution*. New York: Simon and Schuster.

———. 1975. "Are lesbians 'gay'?" *Ms*. 3(12):86.

Kimmel, Michael and Michael Messner, eds. 1992. *Men's Lives*, Second Edition. Mew York: MacMillan.

Kinsey, Alfred, et al. 1948. *Sexual Behavior in the Human Male*. Philadelphia: W.B. Saunders.

———. 1953. *Sexual Behavior in the Human Female*. Philadelphia: W.B. Saunders.

Kinsman, Gary. 1992. "Homophobia among men." In *Men's Lives*, 2nd ed., edited by Michael Kimmel and Michael Messner. New York: MacMillan.

Kitzinger, Celia. 1987. *The Social Construction of Lesbianism*. London: Sage.

———. 1993. *Changing Our Minds: Lesbian Feminism and Psychology*. New York: New York University Press.

LaBarbera, Peter. 1993a. "Helping gays 'come out' of homosexuality." *Lambda Report* 1(4):11.

———. 1993b. "Latest findings on 'genetic homosexuality' inconclusive." *Lambda Report* 1(4):5.

Levine, Martin. 1979. "Gay ghetto." In *Gay Men: The Sociology of Male Homosexuality*, edited by Martin Levine. New York: Harper Colophon.

Lewis, Sasha. 1979. *Sunday's Women*. Boston: Beacon.

McIntosh, Mary. 1981. "The homosexual role." In *The Making of the Modern Homosexual*, edited by Kenneth Plummer. London: Hutchinson.

Maggenti, Maria. 1991. "Women as queer nationals." *Out/Look* No.11:20–23.

———. 1993. "Wandering through Herland." In *Sisters, Sexperts, Queers*, edited by Arlene Stein. New York: Plume.

Marcus, Eric. 1993. *Is It a Choice? Answers to 300 of the Most Frequently Asked Questions About Gays and Lesbians*. San Francisco: Harper.

Martin, Del and Phyllis Lyon. 1972. *Lesbian/Woman*. New York: Bantam.

Mills, C. Wright. 1940. "Situated actions and vocabularies of motive." *American Sociological Review* 5(6):904–13.

———. 1959. *The Sociological Imagination*. New York: Oxford University Press.

Minkowitz, Donna. 1992. "See what the girls in the backroom will have." *Village Voice*, June 30:34,38.

———. 1993. "Trial by science." *Village Voice*, November 30:27–29.

Moraga, Cherrie and Gloria Anzaldua, eds. 1983. *This Bridge Called My Back*. New York: Kitchen Table.

Nardi, Peter. 1993. "Gays should lean on justice, not science." *Los Angeles Times*, August 6:B7.

Newton, Esther. 1984. "The mythic mannish lesbian: Radclyffe Hall and the new woman." *Signs* 9: 557–75.

———. 1988. "Of yams, grinders, and gays." *Out/Look* 1(1):29–37.

————, and Shirley Walton. 1984. "The misunderstanding: Toward a more precise sexual vocabulary." In *Pleasure and Danger: Exploring Female Sexuality*, edited by Carole Vance. New York: Routledge.

Omi, Michael and Howard Winant. 1994. *Racial Formation in the United States*, second edition. New York: Routledge.

Paglia, Camille. 1994. "Where gay boys come from." *The Harvard Gay and Lesbian Review* Spring 1994:4–7.

Penelope, Julia and Susan Wolfe, eds. 1989. *The Original Coming Out Stories*. Freedom, Calif.: Crossing Press.

Peper, Karen. 1993. "To choose or not to change: Challenging the *NY Times*/CBS News poll on homosexuality." *Deneuve*, July/August:10–11.

Phelan, Shane. 1989. *Identity Politics: Lesbian Feminism and the Limits of Community*. Philadelphia: Temple University Press.

Plummer, Kenneth. 1981. "Homosexual categories." In *The Making of the Modern Homosexual*, edited by Kenneth Plummer. London: Hutchinson.

————. 1992. "Speaking its name: Inventing a lesbian and gay studies." In *Modern Homosexualities*, edited by Kenneth Plummer. London: Routledge.

Ponse, Barbara. 1978. *Identities in the Lesbian World: The Social Construction of Self*. Westport, Conn.: Greenwood Press.

Rabey, Steve. 1993. "Amendment 2's legality tested in Denver court." *Christianity Today*, November 22:41.

Radicalesbians. 1992. "The woman-identified woman." In *Out of the Closets: Voices of Gay Liberation*, edited by Karla Jay and Allen Young. New York: New York University Press.

Reback, Cathy. 1986. "Constructions of a 'real' lesbian." Paper presented at the annual meetings of the American Sociological Association, New York, September 1986.

Reiss, Albert. 1961. "The social integration of peers and queers." *Social Problems* 9:102–30.

The Report. 1993. "The Gay Agenda" (video). Lancaster, California.

Rich, Adrienne. 1980. "Compulsory heterosexuality and lesbian existence." *Signs*, 5:631–60.

Rosenfels, Paul. 1971. *Homosexuality: The Psychology of the Creative Process*. New York: Ninth Street Center.

Ross, Michael. 1980. "Retrospective distortion in homosexual research." *Archives of Sexual Behavior* 9:523–31.

Rubin, Gayle. 1981. "The leather menace: Comments on politics and s/m." In *Coming to Power*, edited by SAMOIS. Boston: Alyson Publications.

Rust, Paula. 1991. "Neutralizing the political threat of the marginal woman: Lesbians' beliefs about bisexual women." Paper presented at the annual meetings of the American Sociological Association, Cincinnati.

Sagarin, Edward. 1976. "Prison homosexuality and its effects on post-prison sexual behavior." *Journal of Health and Social Behavior* 9:177–85.

Schmalz, Jeffrey. 1993. "Poll finds an even split on homosexuality's cause." *New York Times* March 5:A14.

Schur, Edwin. 1979. *Interpreting Deviance*. New York: Harper and Row.

———. 1980. *The Politics of Deviance.* Englewood Cliffs: Prentice–Hall.

———. 1984. *Labeling Women Deviant.* New York: Random House.

———. 1988. *The Americanization of Sex.* Philadelphia: Temple University.

Scott, Martin B. and S. M. Lyman. 1968. "Accounts." *American Sociological Review* 33:46–62.

Sedgwick, Eve Kosofsky. 1990. *Epistemology of the Closet.* Berkeley: University of California Press.

Seidman, Steven. "Identity and politics in a 'postmodern' gay culture: Some historical and conceptual notes." In *Fear of a Queer Planet,* edited by Michael Warner. Minneapolis: University of Minnesota Press.

———. 1994. "Symposium: Queer theory/sociology: A dialogue." *Sociological Theory* 12:166–177.

———. 1992. "How to bring your kids up gay." *Social Text* 9:19–27.

Simon, William and John Gagnon. 1967. "Femininity in the lesbian community." *Social Problems* 15:212–21.

Smith, Barbara, ed., 1983. *Home Girls: A Black Feminist Anthology.* New York: Kitchen Table Press.

Smith-Rosenberg, Carroll. 1989. "Discourses of sexuality and subjectivity." In *Hidden From History: Reclaiming the Gay and Lesbian Past,* edited by Martin Duberman, Martha Vicinus, and George Chauncey, Jr. New York: Meridian.

Snitow, Ann, Christine Stansell and Sharon Thompson, 1983. *Powers of Desire.* New York: Monthly Review.

———. 1990. "A gender diary." In *Conflicts in Feminism,* edited by Marianne Hirsch and Evelyn Fox Keller. New York: Routledge.

Starbuck, Gene. 1981. *Models of Human Sexuality and Social Control.* Washington, D.C.: University Press of America. Stein, Arlene. 1992. "Sisters and queers: The decentering of lesbian feminism." *Socialist Review* 22:33–55.

Stein, Arlene. 1992. "Sisters and queers: The decentering of lesbian feminism." *Socialist Review* 22:33–55.

———. 1993. "The year of the lustful lesbian." In *Sisters, Sexperts, Queers: Beyond the Lesbian Nation,* edited by Arlene Stein. New York: Plume.

——— and Ken Plummer. 1994. "'I can't even think straight': Queer theory and the missing sexual revolution in sociology." *Sociological Theory* 12:178–187.

Troiden, Richard. 1988. *Lesbian and Gay Identity: A Sociological Analysis.* Dix Hills, N.Y.: General Hall, Inc.

Udis-Kessler, Amanda. 1991. "Present tense: Biphobia as a crisis of meaning." In *Bi Any Other Name: Bisexual People Speak Out,* edited by Loraine Hutchins and Lani Kaahumanu. Boston: Alyson Publications.

Valverde, Mariana. 1991. "As if subjects existed: Analysing social discourses." *Canadian Review of Sociology and Anthropology* 28:173–87.

Van Buren, Abby. 1993. "Deathbed promise must be kept, reader says." *Tulsa World* February 23:C2.

Van Gelder, Lindsy. 1991. "The 'born that way' trap." *Ms.*, May/June:86–87.

Weeks, Jeffrey. 1977. *Coming Out.* London: Quartet.

———. 1981. *Sex, Politics and Society.* London: Longman.

————. 1985. *Sexuality and its Discontents*. London: Routledge and Kegan Paul.

Weinberg, Martin S. and Colin J. Williams. 1974. *Male Homosexuals*. New York: Oxford University.

Weinberg, Thomas S. 1978. "On doing and being gay." *Journal of Homosexuality* 4:143–56.

————. 1983. *Gay Men, Gay Selves: The Social Construction of Homosexual Identities*. New York: Irvington.

Whisman, Vera. 1986. "The social construction of sexuality: An exploratory study." Paper presented at the annual meetings of the American Sociological Association, New York.

————. 1992. "Identity crises: Who is a lesbian, anyway?" In *Sisters, Sexperts, Queers*, edited by Arlene Stein. New York: Plume.

————. 1994. "The seams in our constructions: AIDS in the history of lesbian self-definition." In *A Plague of Our Own: The Impact of the AIDS Epidemic on Gay Men and Lesbians*. Chicago: University of Chicago Press.

Whitam, Frederick. 1977. "Childhood indicators of male homosexuality." *Archives of Sexual Behavior* 6:89–96.

———— and Robin Mathy. 1985. *Male Homosexuality in Four Societies*. New York: Praeger.

Wittman, Carl. 1992. "Refugees from Amerika: A gay manifesto." In *Out of the Closets: Voices of Gay Liberation*, edited by Karla Jay and Allen Young. New York: New York University Press.

Wolf, Deborah Goleman. 1980. *The Lesbian Community*. Berkeley: University of California.

Wood, Mary. 1993. "A question of choice: Versions of how we got that way." *Center for the Study of Women in Society Review*, University of Oregon.

Yearly, Steven. 1988. "Settling accounts: Action, accounts and sociological explanation." *The British Journal of Sociology* 34:578–99.

Zicklin, Gilbert. 1992. "Re-biologizing sexual orientation: A critique." Paper presented at the Annual Meetings of the Society for the Study of Social Problems, Pittsburg, August.

Zita, Jacquelyn. 1981. "Historical amnesia and the lesbian continuum." *Signs* 7:172–87.

Index